GLOBAL

ASPIRATIONS

AND THE

REALITY OF

CHANGE

how can we do things differently?

GLOBAL ASPIRATIONS AND THE REALITY OF CHANGE

how can we do things differently?

Edited by Harry Bohan and Gerard Kennedy

our society in
the new millennium

VERITAS

First published 2004 by
Veritas Publications
7/8 Lower Abbey Street
Dublin 1
Ireland
Email publications@veritas.ie
Website www.veritas.ie

ISBN 1 85390 742 1

'St Kevin and the Blackbird' and 'At the Wellhead', both from the The Spirit
Level, and extract from 'Triptych II – Sibyl', from New Selected Poems 1966-1987,
all by Seamus Heaney; used by permission of Faber & Faber Ltd. 'Hazelnuts'
by Moya Cannon from The Parchment Boat (1997) used by kind permission of
the author and The Gallery Press. 'Fill Arís' and 'Ní Ceadmhach Neamhshuim'
by Séan Ó Ríordáin; © Caoimhín Ó Marcaigh / Sairseal Ó Marcaigh.
'Everybody Sang' by Siegfried Sassoon © Siegfried Sassoon; used by kind
permission of George Sassoon.

Cover by Avid Design
Printed in the Republic of Ireland by Betaprint Ltd, Dublin

CONTENTS

CONTRIBUTORS

John Quinn is a well-known broadcaster who retired from RTÉ Radio in December 2002 after a career of twenty-five years, during which he won various awards in Ireland, Tokyo and New York. An established writer of children's fiction (he won the Bisto Book of the Year Award in 1992), he has also edited several other acclaimed publications. In February 2003, he was awarded an honorary D. Litt by the University of Limerick.

Mícheál Ó Súilleabháin is best known as a performer who has developed a uniquely Irish piano style. His composition and music performance activity is mirrored in his work as an ethnomusicologist. From 1975 to 1993 he worked in the Music Department of University College, Cork, with young traditional and classical musicians from Ireland, the UK and North America. In that time, he established UCC Music Department as the first such educational body to work towards the integration of traditional and classical musicians within a shared curriculum. In January 1994 he continued this work at postgraduate level in the University of Limerick, where he was appointed the first holder of a new Chair of Music, and founded the Irish World Music Centre. Since his initial recording on the Gael Linn label in 1975 (re-issued in CD format in 1991) his main recordings include *Cry of the Mountain*

(Gael Linn, 1982) and seven recordings in a series with the Virgin/Venture label. His most recent album, *Templum,* was released in Autumn 2001.

Michael Cronin was educated at Trinity College, Dublin and University College, Dublin. He taught in the University of Tours and the École Normale Supérieure (Cachan, France) before returning to Ireland in the mid-1980s. He is currently Director of the Centre for Translation Studies and Textual Studies, Dublin City University and co-editor of *The Irish Review.* As an author and lecturer, Michael Cronin has explored the relationship between culture, language and identity both within Ireland and on a global scale. He has also investigated the effects of mobility on society and understanding of self and the political challenges facing a radically transformed Irish society. His publications include *Translating Ireland: Translation, Languages, Identities* (Cork University Press, 1996), *Across the Lines: Travel, Language and Translation* (Cork University Press, 2000), and as co-editor, *Tourism in Ireland: A Critical Analysis* (Cork University Press, 1993) and *Reinventing Ireland: Culture, Society and the Global Economy* (Pluto Press, 2002). His current publications include *Irish Tourism, Image, Culture and Identity* (Channel View Publications) co-edited with Barbra O'Connor and *Translation and Globalization* (Routledge, 2003). This book examines new translation paradigms as determined by global societies and economies.

Melanie Verwoerd was born in Pretoria, South Africa. In the early 1980s, she began her studies for a BA degree in theology in Stellenbosch University and went on to receive an MA degree in Feminist Theology in 1996. During her visit to Oxford in 1986, Ms Verwoerd began making links with political organisations and on her return to South Africa in 1990, became a member of the ANC. In 1994 she was elected as ANC Member of Parliament, making her the youngest female member. From 1998 to 2001 Ms Verwoerd resided in Cape Town and served as a Member of Parliament representing the ANC. During her seven years in parliament she visited Holland, Australia, Cuba, Sweden, Chile, Brazil, the USA, Taiwan, Israel and Ireland as a member of fact-finding teams. Ms Verwoerd also visited London to support the asbestos victims in their court case against Cape Plc. In March 2001 Ms Verwoerd was appointed South African Ambassador to Ireland. She is married to Wilhelm and they have two children.

Sinéad Donnelly, MD, FRCPI, is a consultant in Palliative Medicine with the Mid Western Health Board since January 2000. Dr Donnelly is responsible for the care of people who have advanced, progressive illnesses, such as cancer, within the Mid West region. Dr Donnelly worked previously in Scotland, the United States and in Our Lady's Hospice, Dublin. She has a particular interest in qualitative research and its application to palliative care as well as traditions in Ireland associated with care of the sick and dying in the past. Arising from this work, Dr Donnelly produced a documentary, *Anam*, which was shown on TG4 in October 2002. This year a second documentary is in progress, which describes how families with a member with a serious illness cope with the support of the community; this community being family, friends and neighbours as well as professional carers. The working title for this documentary is *Meitheal* and it is hoped that it will be broadcast nationally in the near future.

Ged Pierse is one of the leading figures in Irish commercial and sporting life. He is the chairman and founder of Pierse Contracting, which is one of Ireland's largest construction and development companies. In addition, he is a promoter and director of many of the new landmark commercial and residential developments that have reshaped the Irish landscape. Pierse Contracting is a major contributor to the Irish business scene employing directly over six hundred and fifty people. Such landmark developments as the East Point Office Park in Dublin's docklands and the Citibank Building, the National College of Ireland and Clarion Quay projects are examples of the Pierse hallmark. His company was given charge of the restoration and redevelopment of the historic Government Buildings in Merrion Row in Dublin and has also completed many large-scale public works projects. A civil engineer by profession, Ged lives in Dublin with his wife Paula. They have four daughters and eight grandchildren. At sixty-one Ged Pierse is a devoted family man, an energetic sportsman, an appreciative sponsor of educational and literary endeavour and a person of boundless energy, determination and commitment to the development of modern Ireland.

Paula Downey is a partner at downey youell associates, the Dublin-based organisational development practice working at the critical intersection of communication, values and culture to improve the processes and practices that enable an organisation to get in touch and stay in touch with itself and its values, and the needs and values of its wider community of interest. Having spent twenty years at senior management level, Paula is particularly interested in the changing relationship between business and society, and the urgent need for business to demonstrate leadership in response to the pressing and complex issues of our generation. She is currently engaged in a project to measure the values of business, the first study of its kind in Ireland. In addition to speaking and writing on these topics, Paula brings her passion to The Communication Dynamic, a unique range of learning and development programmes designed to trigger fresh thinking about our influence and responsibility as individuals and organisations. She is co-author of *Exploring the Communication Dynamic – 301 Building Blocks to Enrich your Working Relationships* (1998). She has a distinction in Communication Studies and a

Masters Degree in Responsibility and Business Practice from the University of Bath.

Padraig O'Ceidigh is the MD of Aer Arann and also the MD of *Foinse,* the national Irish-language weekly newspaper. He has worked as an accountant and is a qualified solicitor. Padraig also owns his own printing company, Clodoirí Lurgan Teo., along with a summer language college. In 1994 he purchased Aer Arann. In just a few years Padraig has transformed the traditional local island air service into the world's fastest-growing regional airline, now carrying as many passengers in one week as it did for the entire year in 1998. The airline now employs nearly three hundred people and operates over four hundred flights per week. Padraig's achievements were recognised recently when he was awarded the Ernst & Young Entrepreneur of the Year Award 2002. He went on to represent Ireland at the World Entrepreneur of the Year Awards in Monte Carlo in June 2003.

Jim Power joined Friends First Group in 2000 as Chief Economist and Director of Investment Strategy. He is a non-executive director and investment consultant to F&C (Ireland) Limited, the Irish asset management arm of the pan-European Eureko Group, of which Friends First is part. He worked for the AIB group from 1979 to 1991 in Retail Banking, Strategic Planning and Group Treasury, where he was the Treasury Economist. He joined Bank of Ireland in 1991 as Senior Economist. He was appointed Chief Economist in 1995, and a Director in Treasury and International in 1998. He is a frequent contributor to Irish and UK media. He holds a BA in Economics and Politics, and a Master of Economic Science Degree from University College, Dublin. He currently lectures in Finance at Dublin City University. He recently sat on the Competitiveness Expert Group, within the Enterprise Strategy Group set up in August 2003 by the Minister for Enterprise, Trade and

Employment to advise and make recommendations on Ireland's future policy options for encouraging and generating growth and employment in the economy. Jim Power is a native of Waterford and is married with two young sons.

FOREWORD

Harry Bohan

Globalisation is a term widely used to describe the ongoing process of increasing economic, cultural, political and environmental interaction. It is driven by extraordinary technological progress, especially in the fields of information, communication and transport, and by political decisions to open up and deregulate markets. It would seem that the trend towards deepening global interdependence is now irreversible.

This process brings about fundamental change to the way society is organised. It creates new opportunities for people around the globe, including those in developing countries. It is inevitable, however, that in the context of these major and rapid changes new pressures of adjustment will arise in both the industrialised and developing world.

Notwithstanding the remarkable success of the world economy at the beginning of the twenty-first century (Ireland has been a major beneficiary), the vicious circle of stagnation and poverty in the poorest countries remains unbroken. And there is then the question of how the institutions of social life and local culture are responding. In Ireland, two of the great examples of the local responding to the global are in the areas of music and dance. Irish music and dance are now prominent on the world stage.

But, in general, as the pace of change continues to accelerate it would seem that the process of human development is, in comparison, achingly slow. There are indications that material culture is being transformed faster than the human qualities to do with relationships, the way we behave, the way we govern ourselves. Economies change fast, societies take time to change. When the external world is changing faster than the inner world our environment can become bewildering and threatening. An indication of this is the fact that the security industry is experiencing such fast growth. The question of trust has become a major issue.

Some of these issues have been highlighted at previous Céifin Conferences. Certainly a theme running through a number of contributions has been summed up in the words of Peter Russell: 'The next great frontier for human development is not outer space, but inner space.' (see *Is The Future My Responsibility? – Our Society in the New Millennium*, 2001 Céifin Conference papers)

The focus of the 2003 conference was to put more emphasis on action and how we translate analysis into reality. As change is at the heart of this process, the conference focused on exploring the dynamics of change. The panel of national and international speakers offered an insight into change that has taken place in local and global worlds and provided practical examples of supporting change by doing things differently.

I would like to thank each of the speakers: Micheál Ó Súilleabháin, Michael Cronin, Sinead Donnelly, Paula Downey, Ged Pierse, Melanie Verwoerd, Padraig O'Ceidigh, and particularly Jim Power who stepped into the breach at very short notice. A special thank you to our chair people, Anne Taylor, Fintan O'Toole and John Quinn.

On behalf of Céifin, I offer my congratulations to Tom Hyland, the recipient of the 2003 Céifin Values-Led Change Award. This award is merited for his work in highlighting awareness of East Timor and becoming one of the founder members of the East Timor Ireland Solidarity Campaign.

We are deeply grateful for the ongoing support of our sponsors, ESB, Waterford Crystal, West County Hotel and Gilbeys. I would also like to pay a special tribute to all our volunteers; this conference would not be possible without their support. Finally I would like to thank the Céifin staff and RRD staff for their commitment to making this conference a huge success.

Harry Bohan
February 2004

JUST IMAGINING!

John Quinn

Just imagine experiencing a feast of story ideas, dialogue, music, drama and good conversation …

Just imagine you grew up in comfort and seclusion in a divided South Africa, then rejected all you had been taught and became an ANC activist and MP. Then imagine your President Nelson Mandela sent you as Ambassador to Ireland, suggesting you continue to be an activist, but a discreet and diplomatic one! Imagine you are Melanie Verwoerd. What stories, what hope you could bring with you!

Just imagine you are a world-class musician and professor of music. What a vision of the 'lobal' (local and global) influences that music, poetry, the arts might bring to a fractured world. Imagine you could sing the words of Heaney and Ó Riordáin to illustrate that vision. 'Indifference will not be allowed'. Imagine the challenge of those five words! Just imagine weaving the magic fiddling of an eighty-four-year-old Clare farmer with the vibrant voices and drums of Congolese natives! Imagine the richness of that weave!

Just imagine in the space of forty minutes being transported through the revolution that Ireland has experienced in the past decade – the rise and rise in consumption, the acceleration in the pace of work and personal life, the effect of communication replacing transmission, the means overcoming the end ... but despite all that, imagine that change is possible. Imagine a revolution of deceleration ...

Just imagine facing up to the greatest change of all in our human lives – the termination of that life by a ravaging disease. Imagine you are a young doctor involved in palliative care, accompanying patients and their families on their final journeys. What heart-rending stories you could tell – stories of dignity and hope!

And imagine you are a captain of industry – in this instance the construction industry – viewing with great unease the changing world you see about you. A world ravaged by corruption, drugs, alcohol, social breakdown – a world that cries out for trust, values, love.

Just imagine having a whole morning to reflect on the possibilities of influencing the system of power that keeps us politically docile and economically productive. Imagine having a facilitator like Paula Downey open your mind to the liberating notion of moving from 'power over' to 'power with' and 'power within'. Imagine the joy of realising that power is present in every moment, in every relationship and there is ultimately no 'small act' ....

Just imagine being energised and upset by an economist's view of globalisation's beneficial effects on our economy ....

And imagine you are a discontented young teacher who goes for a walk on Christmas Day and looking at an airstrip in a Connemara bog, you develop a wonderful vision of building an airline. Imagine the story you could tell ...

Just imagine all that and the camaraderie and the energy of spending two days with three hundred people who want to do things differently, who want to effect change. Imagine conversations – at early and late hours – with a Cork dairy farmer who is 'into reading and studying theology', with a Belfast-based worker with the disabled on the themes of imagination and daydreaming; with a County Galway publican on his dream of revitalising his own and other villages ...

Stories, dreams, ideas, debate, energy, conversations. Power within. Céifin 2003. Just imagine!

LISTENING TO DIFFERENCE
IRELAND IN A WORLD OF MUSIC

Mícheál Ó Súilleabháin

Listening to the River

While I was preparing this talk the Irish phrase came to me: *'píobaire an aon phort'* meaning 'the piper with only one tune!' It is a derogatory reference to someone who has only one song to sing. But for the past few years I have found myself speaking to public gatherings in a wide variety of settings – and saying what may well be the same thing, although I hope at least saying it in different ways. If what I say this evening hovers in the realms of the poetic then bear with me as I attempt to ground the poetic with poetry itself. Translating that poetry into action is quite another matter – and the aim of this sixth Céifin Conference is, after all, to put more emphasis on action. Nonetheless, while I have my own ideas as to how that can be done, in certain arenas and instances at least, I will happily leave that process to what follows at this conference over the next few days. My hope, at any rate, is that my words may provide some point of general reference, and may encourage us into a receptive mood for what is to follow.

After all, the Russian composer, Stravinsky, said of Vivaldi's music that he wrote one good piece and kept repeating it, which is one way of looking at it – or at least listening to it. Or we might think of the example where people hear traditional music in Ireland from their own perspective, and wonder how musicians can sit and play what seems to them to be the same tune all night!

And this is what I mean then in my title – 'Listening to Difference'. It usually takes some concentration and some learning to focus the ear – much as the eye can focus – and thus to start the process of noticing the little differences which make a big difference. Mind you, in the absence of the concentration and learning, it is heartening in my experience that a little bit of common sense, even on its own, goes quite a long way.

Basically, the message these words are intended to bring is that there *is* hope, that there *is* light and that the struggle for an active peace on this multi-coloured planet that we share is well worth making. And I suppose that is what Céifin is all about – seeking out the value of human existence and holding it up like a light for all to see. 'Look!' it says. 'Here is a light on the banks of the Shannon in the county of Clare in the west of Ireland. It is our light. It is our contribution to a world of lights. And within our light there is a world of different lights. And within that world of different lights there is a shared brightness, a luminosity that penetrates the darkness and heralds yet another dawn. And Nature teaches us that it doesn't only happen once. It has to happen every day like a birthing, or like a spring at the source of a river.' For that reason, we need to listen to the river.

Éist le fuaim na habhann agus gheobhair breac.

'Listen to the sound of the river and you will get a trout', the Irish proverb tells us. I want to bring you on a journey up that river to its source where we will find the inspiration, which was the remit of Céibhfhionn, the early Celtic Goddess for whom this organisation is named. In order to make that journey I will make use of poetry, music and language – all three linked as sound as we listen to the river.

I start with St Kevin of Glendalough, and our opening scene shows him fasting during Lent with his two arms outstretched.

His cell is so small that his hands are out through the windows
on either side, or a bird nests in one of his upturned palms.
Here is how Seamus Heaney captures it[1]:

St Kevin and the Blackbird

And then there was St Kevin and the blackbird.
The saint is kneeling, arms stretched out, inside
His cell, the cell is narrow, so

One turned up palm is out the window, stiff
As a crossbeam, when a blackbird lands
And lays in it and settles down to nest.

Kevin feels the warm eggs, the small breast, the tucked
Neat head and claws and, finding himself linked
Into the network of eternal life,

Is moved to pity: now he must hold his hand
Like a branch out in the sun and rain for weeks
Until the young are hatched and fledged and flown.

And since the whole thing's imagined anyhow,
Imagine being Kevin. Which is he?
Self-forgetful or in agony all the time

From the neck on out down through his hurting
forearms?
Are his fingers sleeping? Does he feel his knees?
Or has the shut-eyed blank of underearth

Crept up through him? Is there distance in his head?
Alone and mirrored clear in love's deep river,
'To labour and not to seek reward,' he prays,

> A prayer his body makes entirely
> For he has forgotten self, forgotten bird
> And on the riverbank, forgotten the river's name.

The river's name of course for us here is the Shannon, the longest river, named for the early Irish Goddess Sionna who sought out the hazelnuts of wisdom which in ancient Ireland were believed to contain '*éigse*', the spirit and inspiration of poetry.

Sionna was seeking what Céifin had. This she found next to a pool – the well of knowledge – which was surrounded by nine hazel trees. The hazel is linked to autumn and to the festival of Samhain. As the ripe nuts fall into the water they burst into a purple spray. The salmon of wisdom who live in the pool eat the nuts and for every nut they eat, a red spot appears on their skin. The nuts also cause bubbles of inspiration in the water, which are constantly carried downstream. Sionna leans over the pool to gather the nuts, but loses her footing and falls in. The pool is angered and rises up over her and sweeps her down into the sea, thus birthing the river, which still carries her name.

The hazelnut, with its round hard shell and nutritious core is a symbol of the heart in many folk tales. Thus, Findabair's heart broke like a nut inside her when she heard of her father's death in battle. And Acaill wept for nine days until her heart broke like a nut inside her when she heard of the death of her brother, Erc[2].

The poet, Moya Cannon, expertly marks the connection with the heart as a hazelnut of wisdom:

Hazelnuts

I thought that I knew what they meant
when they said that wisdom is a hazelnut.
You have to search the scrub
for hazel thickets,
gather the ripened nuts,

crack the hard shells,
and only then taste the sweetness at wisdom's kernel.

But perhaps it is simpler.
Perhaps it is we who wait in thickets
for fate to find us
and break us between its teeth
before we can start to know anything.

Another part of the necessary wisdom of the times we live in, and a wisdom which is surely at the heart of Céifin's concern, is an understanding of the dynamic between the local and the global[3]. How do we make the movement between what we were, what we are, and what we are becoming? Listening to the difference between the local and the global is like listening to the difference between self and other.

The Art of Listening[4]

Music is the Art of Listening. And my musings here are about the Art of Listening, in particular the Art of Global Listening. Whenever we respectively cross the boundaries that border our musical experience from that of another, we move something on. Every movement of respectful knowing we make creates another stepping stone where someone may follow – or indeed someone may come across from the other side.

I find my text again in Heaney where he reminds us that for the Romans, Terminus was the God of Boundaries, and that the image of Terminus, which they kept in the Temple of Jupiter on Capitol Hill, had no roof and was open to the sky. This was redolent of the *templum* or sacred space where the future might be foretold. The word *templum* originally stood for that section of the sky where the stars might be read or the movement of birds be observed. Later it came to mean that particular space on which you stood while speculating the stars. And indeed the word *terminus* appears in Irish as *tearmann*, which is found in many Irish place names 'meaning the glebe land belonging to an abbey or church, land that was specially marked off for ecclesiastical use'.⁵ How we enter and exit the sacred space of listening and of speculation seems important. The Entrance Hymn and the Recessional are key moments in the ritual. In 1994 while writing the music of *Missa Gadelica*⁶, a poem came to me as if to put me on alert to find the point 'where light and waters meet'. I found myself using it as the inspiration for 'meditation music', which was to prepare the listening congregation for the moment of crossing.

Templum
The sea is a temple.
Vested in seaweed,
Priestly fish find coral waters.
Undercurrents beat time.
Overhead, where light and waters meet,
Blind ships take soundings.
My temples are riverbanks for the templum of the sea.
Poor pilot,
I stand at the crown of my sacred vessel
Trusting the North star,
Journeying home.

We can take the idea further into another Irish word – not related but all the stronger for that – the word *táirseach*, meaning threshold. This is the word for the lintel of a door, the boundary between the inner and the outer world, between the local and the global. It is a place of great creativity and fertility. Folklore in Ireland has it that Saint Bridgit, whose feast day on 1 February marks the beginning of spring and of the agricultural year, was born with her mother having one leg inside the threshold of the door and the other without. Based upon an earlier Celtic Goddess called Ainu, St Bridgit is an earth goddess and a keeper of the flame of creativity. St

Bridgit's flame, which was kept alight in her monastery in Kildare, is the light to mark the passage of those of us who are drawn towards the borders of difference. It is the light of knowledge and of true understanding, which comes through a studied listening. And above all it is the light of respectful listening. A listening at the borders of difference.

Terminus of course also carries the meaning of an end of something. We speak of being terminally ill. Or of something being terminated. It is as if the various slantings of the word are telling us that an end is also potentially a beginning. There is a mystery and an accompanying obstacle of darkness, therefore, which may accompany a boundary crossing which is why we need the light of creativity to see us through, to keep us, as it were, safe and sound.

The musical challenge we face in our own times is to address the global multiplicity of voices as never before. To continue to work like a good cartographer drawing the educational map of the location of the stepping-stones. Everyone must find them in the end for themselves for the experience to be as wholesome as it should be, and everyone *will* find them in their own way and at their own rate – something that must also be respected. But as mediators or leaders, or facilitators, our task is to hold the light steady for the duration of the passing to and through the *terminus* or the *tearmann*. And to pass from what I call the *tempus* (that which is finite) to the *templum* and back again, and in this way to go beyond the metronome of existence to the cantabile, or singing, of understanding.

We do it with our feet on the ground and our heads in the clouds, and with our eyes closed. Heaney quotes the seventeenth-century Japanese poet Basho[7]:

> What is important is to keep our mind high in the world of true understanding, and returning to the world of daily experience to seek therein the truth of beauty. No matter what we may be doing at a given moment, we

must not forget that it has a bearing upon our everlasting
self, which is poetry.

It is this ability of music, and of the arts in general, to encode
connections that links its intelligence with the intelligence at
the heart of politics and at the heart of identity itself. And it is
this power within music to encapsulate, represent, and at times
actually *be* at the quick of things, which sets it up as a potential
barometer of the times. This may also be the reason why
people within a culture can react so deeply when music
changes. Music, and the other arts, can at times reside at the
crossroads of becoming where the dynamic of cultural change
is being generated. The current debate within Irish culture
about the speed and nature of change within traditional music
is a case in point.[8]

Edward Said in *Culture and Imperialism*[9]:

> No one can deny the persisting continuities of long
> traditions, sustained habitations, national languages, and
> cultural geographies, but there seems no reason except
> fear and prejudice to keep insisting on their separateness
> and distinctiveness as if that was all human life was
> about. Survival in fact is about the connection between
> things.

The Lobality of the World

The balance between *locus* and *globus* is a key to unlocking
those connections, the key to the music within, the key to
making the body of a culture start to sing again. Linking the
local to the global may be something of a cliché now, but it is
one that remains pregnant with meaning and relevance. As an
example of this, my attention was recently drawn to a 'cultural
village' architectural concept, which the Italian architect Renzo
Piano designed for New Caledonia off the coast of Australia. It
is a strikingly beautiful series of buildings based on the local

tribal huts of the Kanak people. Someone once described this kind of architecture, which was at once local and global as 'glocal'. As I thought about the world – especially its hardness and almost musical aggression – I was drawn towards a different amalgamation of the two words 'local'/'global' into 'lobal'. Quite apart from its softness, 'lobal' carries resonances of the lobe of the ear, of a kind of respectful listening, of a capacity to listen to difference.

Because what we might now call 'lobality' listens to the process of becoming, because it is, as T.S. Eliot puts it, the dance 'at the still point of the turning world', because in Yeats's words it 'calls the Muses home', it leads us towards what George Steiner has called 'real presence' – a place where creativity resides. If I put these words together I get this statement;

> The real presence at the crossroads of becoming is the globality of the world turning at the still point of existence.

Here lies the heart of intelligence, the juncture of survival, Said's 'connections between things'.

That combination of fear and prejudice alluded to by Said can short circuit this process. Sometimes the dynamic of a musical tradition can disturb old haunts, challenge established settings, seek to replace old gods. At its worst, the reaction against this can breed a cultural fundamentalism where outrage is tainted by fear. At its best it can help to redress an emerging imbalance within a tradition by counteracting crass commercialism, or by challenging dishonest political manoeuvrings within institutions. It is in finding a balance that a culture reaches towards its healthy aspects, and it is fundamentally within the individual that this balance emerges. The encouragement of choice seems essential to finding that balance. The continual opening up of other ways of doing what has been done before seems to keep tradition alive.

We have to learn to listen for that process. Listening – which is the theme of my talk – is a kind of waiting, a kind of suspended alertness which, again, Eliot tells us will be found, 'At the still point of the turning world.'

The Deafness of Indifference

I want to take as my text here at this point two poems by the twentieth-century Irish language poet Seán Ó Ríordáin – one insisting on the local, the other insisting on the global. The central question is raised, therefore, as to whether you can have both? My experience as a musician is that you can. The very contradiction at the heart of the equation is what drives the dynamo. The contradiction is its own answer. And the emergency, which powers that answer, is human creativity.

In the poem 'Fill Arís' (Return Again) Ó Ríordáin tells us to head westwards towards the Dingle peninsula where the Irish language is for him the hazelnut of wisdom:

Téir faobhar na faille siar tráthnóna gréine go Corca
Dhuibhne,
Is chífir thiar ag bun na spéire ag ráthaíocht ann
An Uimhir Dhé, is an Modh Foshuiteach,
Is an tuiseal gairmeach ar bhéalaibh daoine:
Sin é do dhoras,
Dún Chaoin fé sholas an tráthnóna.
Buail is osclófar
D'intinn féin is do chló ceart.

If we get there, he tells us, we will find at the sky's edge the play of language on people's lips. The village of Dun Chaoin lit by an evening sun will be outdoors towards the fingerprint of our own soul. What interests me about this poem, apart from its startling beauty, is a line in it, which says: *Ní dual do neach a thigh ná a threabh a thréighan*. (It is not in the nature of the soul to abandon its home.[10])

Recently I became aware of the other Ó Ríordáin poem, which I want to mention here:

Ní Ceadmhach Neamhshuim

Níl cuil, níl leamhan, níl beach
Dar chruthaigh Dia, níl fear,
Nach dualgas dúinn a leas,
Níl bean; ní ceadmhach neamhshuim
A dhéanamh dá n-imní;
Níl gealt i ngleann na ngealt,
Nár chuí dhúinn suí lena ais,
Á thionlacan an fhaid
A iompraíonn thar ár gceann
Ár dtinneas-ne 'na mheabhair.

Níl áit, níl sruth, níl sceach,
Dá iargúlta iad, níl leac,
Bídís thuaidh, thoir, thiar nó theas,
Nár cheart dúinn machnamh ar a suíomh
Le gean is le báidhíocht;
Dá fhaid uainn Afraic Theas,
Dá airde í gealach,
Is cuid dínn iad ó cheart:
Níl áit ar fuaid na cruinne
Nach ann a saolaíodh sinne.

Here we are told that the only real sin is that of indifference born of fear. Every man, every woman, every living thing, all of nature no matter where it exists is part of our heritage. There is no place on earth where we have not birthed. So we must reconcile the soul's nature to hold to its home with the soul's global birthright. This is the nature of the times we live in. To my mind it can only mean one thing: the local is the global, the home is the planet. But that movement must be achieved with respect to the agricultural reality of our starting point. In the process of this necessary contemporary transformation: indifference. Indifference is not allowed. Compassion, therefore, is necessary. And for compassion to find its voice, you must have global knowledge. And for global knowledge you must have an education system that is beyond commercial and fundamentalist manipulation. You must have a print and electronic media system that is free from interference. In a word, you must have freedom of voice in order to have freedom of choice. Anything else is beneath our human dignity. Anything else is inhuman.

Ó Ríordáin's poem explores the common ground of human heritage. And while that search for common ground is a vital one, we must also search out the boundaries of difference, which unite us as a truly global community.

In one sense, what we *do* is what we *are*. And *how* we do it is *what* we do. Human *doing* is human *being*. And human being is manifest in the rituals of artistic expression in a unique way. We must re-teach ourselves and teach our children how to express themselves. How to find freedom of voice through freedom of choice. This is the heart of the matter. The show of humanity. The saying, the singing, the moving, the sounding, the tracing, the marking, the making – all putting out the human heart on display so that we can be sure again and again that 'all shall be well, and all manner of things shall be well'.

Where the Singing Comes From

The common chessboard of joy, of grief, of hope and shattered hope, of love and disappointment of birthing and of dying – all of these and so much more unite us in our difference, and our difference is held firm in the ritualistic expression of human art and artefact.

The globe spins on its own axis and is ours. It circles the sun. It moves within the solar system through its galaxy. And it races within its galaxy through the universe. Human imagination is as limitless as the mystery of that outer universe, and that imagination finds reflection in the inner world of each human body. These rituals of embodied human communication, in poetry, storytelling, music, dance, in how we chose to build our houses and temples, in how we cultivate the soil – all these speak of an agriculture of the soul, of the inner spark or spirit, of the digging of the humus through the emotional leaves of our lives which we display and shed, and through the ultimate humility which brings us to our knees despite ourselves in the face of life and nature. Eliot, in *Four Quartets*, reminds us that the only wisdom we can hope for is 'the wisdom of humility'.

Is this our search for wisdom? At the well, *within which* if we look deeply enough we can see our reflection in the waters at the bottom? Or if we listen deeply enough we can hear our own voice coming back to us as an echo. We are exiled from our true selves and our lives are a journey back to the beginning all over again. Without even realising it we frantically search for the combination lock which will release even the slightest sighting of ourselves, the merest hint of an echo.

In his poem, 'At the Wellhead'[11], Heaney says:

> Your songs when you sing them with your two eyes closed
> As you always do, are like a local road
> We've known every turn of in the past –
> That midge-veiled, high-hedged side-road where you stood
> Looking and listening until a car
> Would come and go and leave you lonelier
> Than you had been to begin with. So, sing on,
> Dear shut-eyed one, dear far-voiced veteran,
>
> Sing yourself to where the singing comes from...

Yet we stand petrified. We do not know what to do. We do not know where to go. And we do not know whom to turn to. We stand alone on the hilltop of desire, the sun at our backs, the rain in our face, a moon to one side, a tapestry of stars to the other. Around us is an ocean.

Shared artistic ritual allows us to descend into the valleys of artistic communication where fear is assuaged, indifference is outed, and we can be sure once again that even in our aloneness, we are not alone.

We come to love these valleys, these poems, this music, that dance, those places, I, ourselves. We own them as we own up to them. They are our vales of honey, our sun palaces, our bailes and town lands of the familiar, the soundscape of our lives, the landscape of our dreams – a home to go to, a warmth, a comfort, a womb with a view!

These are our traditions, our inheritances, our heritage, things passed through and passed on. They identify us. They are our dynamic selves, the human body out on a limb, the bird singing at the very tip of the branch, the nest left behind for a time for this purpose – to enact and re-enact, to confirm and reconfirm, to tell and retell the human story.

The music of Ireland is such a valley, such a palace, and such a place at the tip of the branch. These soundings on the island can tell us of places of fertility and hope, of wounding, of courage and surprise, and of 'comfortless noises', as when Heaney was visited by a presence during the Northern troubles who spoke through him[12]:

> My people think money
> And talk weather. Oil rigs lull their future
> On single acquisitive stems. Silence
> Has shoaled into the trawlers' echo-sounders.
>
> The ground we kept our ear to for so long
> Is flayed or calloused, and its entrails
> Tented by an impious augury.
> Our island is full of comfortless noises.[13]

Imagine coming back to your own ground like a child, your own valley or mountain, and standing on it to sing out into the heavens so that your voice can be heard right across the world? Imagine if more and more people could do that? Imagine finding that freedom of voice, that freedom of choice, that unlocking of joy, which is our birthright?

The poet Siegfried Sassoon marks such a moment in lines which capture the flight path of what might even be that of the 'hatched and fledged and flown' blackbird which eventually rose out of St Kevin's warm hand in the Heaney poem that we started with. Sassoon is best known as a war poet who documented the misery and duplicity of the First World War. In this poem, 'Everybody Sang', despair gives way to hope, and sadness turns to a joyful vision of completion, of wholeness and wholesomeness, which haunts the human mind as a deeply embedded genetic utopian calling which we cannot and will not leave go of, just as out of the misery of the trenches of war, 'Everybody Sang'[13]:

> Everyone suddenly burst out singing;
> And I was filled with such delight
> As prisoned birds must find in freedom,
> Winging wildly across the white
> Orchards and dark-green fields; on—on—and out
> Of sight.
>
> Everyone's voice was suddenly lifted;
> And beauty came like the setting sun:
> My heart was shaken with tears, and horror
> Drifted away... O, but Everyone
> Was a bird; and the song was wordless; the singing will
> Never be done.

I would like to end this evening with some music[14]. Celebrating difference isn't always about looking outside, or looking across. Sometimes it can be a movement of looking behind, or looking within or to the side. Celebrating difference can sometimes be the same as celebrating tradition. Hearing our own music with new ears. Returning to the wellhead for sustenance.

In order to do that, we do not need to travel vast distances. The wellhead is only up the road.

Notes

1   'St Kevin and the Blackbird' by Seamus Heaney from *The Spirit Level* (Faber and Faber).

2   Niall Mac Coitir, *Irish Trees: Myths, Legends and Folklore*, p. 74 (Cork: The Collins Press 2003).

3   The following section is a development of part of my Sabhal Mór Ostaig Annual Lecture 2002, Isle of Islay, entitled 'The Truth of Beauty: Towards a Global Listening' (in press).

4   Seamus Heaney, *Finders Keepers: Selected Prose 1971-2001*, p. 49.

5   A setting of the mass in Irish, English and Latin commissioned by the Irish Christian Brothers (unpublished 1994).

6   See *Templum*, CD recording by the author (London: Virgin, 2001).

7   Quoted in Heaney, *Finders Keepers*.

8   Fintan Vallelly, ed. *The Crossroads Conference* (Dublin, 1999).

9   Edward Said, *Culture and Imperialism*, p. 408 (London, 1993).

10 Author's free translation.

11 'At the Wellhead' by Seamus Heaney from *The Spirit Level* (Faber and Faber).

12 Extract from 'Triptych II – Sibyl' by Seamus Heaney from *New Selected Poems 1966-1987* (Faber and Faber).

13 Siegfried Sassoon, *The War Poems*, p. 144, (London: Faber and Faber, 1983).

14 The lecture ended with local fiddler Paddy Canny playing tunes to the accompaniment of the author on piano.

HOW THINGS HAVE CHANGED IN IRELAND OVER THE PAST TEN YEARS

Michael Cronin

When I saw the title of my talk, I have to say, I was terrified. The terror has got worse coming close to the lecture because every time people say, 'What are you going to speak about in Clare?' and I answer, 'I am going to speak about how Ireland has changed in the last ten years', they say, 'You're what?' So much has changed in the last ten years that it is difficult to give an account of the extent and scale of those changes. In fact, I was reminded of something I came across recently in a manuscript on Irish travel accounts in the pre-famine period. An anonymous reviewer, writing for what was then called a gentleman's magazine, at the beginning of the nineteenth century, had the following to say on contemplating Ireland's problems. He said 'this was no gratifying duty. The very mention of Ireland conjures up a host of painful recollections and foreboding for which the mind, rather than combat them, would willingly escape. Ireland was like a slumbering volcano, which at any moment in a season of seeming tranquillity may again vomit forth its devastating fires.' I felt a little bit like the reviewer at some point in preparing this lecture. I felt like escape rather than combat, but I liked his image of Ireland as this slumbering volcano, which then gives forth these devastating fires from time to time.

It seems to me that what we have lived through in the last ten years in Ireland is nothing short of revolution. One of the things that characterises revolutionary periods is, of course, the fact that people living in and through them often find it difficult to make sense of what exactly is happening. It is a peculiar kind of revolution, because it is a revolution that hasn't been started or mounted on the barricades. It is a revolution that has been planned in the board rooms. It is a revolution that has been planned in government offices. It is a revolution that has been led and animated by people who, by and large, would not classify themselves as radicals. And yet they changed Irish society in very radical ways.

I want to begin with a couple of figures with which you are probably familiar, but I think it is important to sketch the general framework for what I am going to talk about. Between 1993 and 2001 the annual real growth rate for Ireland was about 8 per cent. In the previous decade the best we could manage was about 3.5 per cent. The numbers at work in the period rose by 45 per cent. Unemployment in the 1980s, if you remember, was around 17 or 18 per cent. Today, it is approximately 4 per cent. In the 1980s, we had the highest net emigration rate in the European Union. We now have one of the highest net immigration rates. Over the last six years, this island has witnessed the arrival of about 250,000 people who have come to live and settle in Ireland.

This, of course, is one set of figures. The set that is often put before us when people are describing what has happened. There are, of course, other sets of figures. The fact that we have the highest level of poverty in the western world, outside of the United States, that the average life expectancy of the Irish male is one of the lowest in the European Union, and that we regularly top new tables when it comes to levels of substance abuse among the young. So these are the two kind of changes, the sort of figures that are often mentioned when people are describing what has happened over the last ten years.

What I would like to concentrate on are changes in Irish society that seem to me less obvious, but that nonetheless have affected us in extremely radical ways. It is what I would call the 'CAC effect'. 'C' for consumption, 'A' for acceleration and 'C' for communication. Let me begin with the notion of consumption. In 1980 a poetry collection by Michael O'Loughlin called *Stalingrad: A Street Dictionary* was published. One of the first poems is called 'Stalingrad', and it sets the mood for the collection. The first two lines are:

> I was born to the stink of whiskey, and failure,
> and a scattered corpse of the real.

What interests me is what is on the cover of that collection. It is a black and white photograph of the PAYE demonstration in 1979 when literally hundreds of thousands of Irish workers took to the streets to complain about the unequal tax burden, which is even more horrifying in the light of recent revelations of malpractice at various levels of Irish society. But what interests me is that the number of producers has grown exponentially in Irish society. That is what this photograph is. It is a photograph of producers on the streets, but in the last decade, despite the fact that the number of producers has grown exponentially, it seems as if the producers have receded from view. In other words, people have increasingly been defined less and less by what they do than by what they consume. Look at television, at the rise in the number of cookery, fashion and home decoration shows, look at the increasing prevalence of property, entertainment, sports, and motoring supplements in all the national newspapers on the island. In other words, one of the arguments I would like to advance here this morning, is that we have moved from a society that was producer-centred to a society that is consumer-centred.

What are the consequences of that shift from production to consumption? If you take consumption, once you buy a good or a service, that is it. The transaction is over from your point of view as a consumer. However, if you look at it from the point of view of production, the experience is radically different, because the difference between consumption and production is that production is a relationship that endures. There are three things that characterise production. One is confidence. The second is trust and the third is obligation. Confidence, because if you produce something, whether it is goods or services, you have to have confidence that what you are making or what you are offering is something that is going to last, that is going to endure. Otherwise you wouldn't do it in the first place. Trust, because when you produce something, or you offer a service, whether it is a case of getting the raw materials, or a case of working with subcontractors, you are indebted to or reliant on other people in order for the good to be produced or the service to be provided. Thirdly, the notion of obligation is the obligation that you sense to the task in hand whether it is production of the good or offering the service, the idea that you will do something to the best of your ability. So these three notions, of confidence, trust and obligation are things that are intrinsic to the production process. So if we have a society that shifts from being production-centred to being consumption-centred, what happens to those notions of confidence, trust and obligation?

There are a number of consequences that have been described by the American sociologist Richard Sennett in describing the American corporate culture. When we think of the extent of American foreign direct investment in Ireland, this too has had palpable effects on many aspects of Irish social and business life. The notion of short term-ism, the lack of confidence in the future, a lack of trust, a certain distrust of others, a kind of 'mé féin-ism', a weakened sense of obligation to the task at hand, which is something that increasingly seems to characterise the working lives of a lot of producers. It was something that was detailed in a report that was produced by the Ceifin Institute last year. If we look at something like personal sector credit, in 1992, 42 per cent of personal disposable income came from personal sector credit. In 2001, that figure had risen to 71 per cent and the figure is rising. Nicholas Boyle, a cultural commentator and a Goethe Scholar, in a book called *Who Are We Now?*, says the following:

> The assumption behind the demand for flexibility in the workers – which denies them the continuity of a fixed identity – is that as consumers too, they will have no fixed or limited desires, not give themselves an identity by voluntarily renouncing any of those desires.

Those desires might include the wish to buy furniture on a Sunday, or to receive forty channels on a TV set. One of the things I want to argue here is that our behaviour as consumers is something that has a direct effect on our lives as producers. Increasingly we have been taught to see ourselves as consumers, not as producers. The problem is that our consumption choices affect the kinds of lives that we can live as producers of goods and services, but it seems to me that a lot of the stress in the workplace and in other areas of life, which has been detailed by so many different groups in society, is to do with the failure to think through properly what our roles as consumers and producers are.

One of the ways in which we can change is to make explicit the link between consumption choices and production consequences and to see how we collectively and socially valorise or highlight the centrality of the production process to our lives. In particular, it seems to me that the networks of dependency in society are important because in an age of individualism, very often what is stressed is the notion of independence, which is seen as a way of rejecting older forms of dependence, but it seems to me that dependence is a crucial position for what should be an ultimate production-centred

value, that of interdependence. A few years ago at the top of
the escalator going to the departures lounge in Dublin airport,
there was an Eircom advertisement. It was a picture of an old
manual telephone exchange and the slogan on it was: 'Stand
still and you're history.' In other words, if you weren't on the
move, if you weren't on the make, you should stay at home and
not be a part of this society. You were a kind of relic of
Christmas past.

There is a very important truth articulated in that Eircom
advert. It is to do with a profound shift in how we are
experiencing our lives which goes back twenty years and is
what I call the shift from geo-politics to chrono-politics. What I
mean by that is that for centuries Ireland's position both
politically and economically tended to be defined by its
geographical position as this small island to the west of the
continental European landmass. So there were problems of
access. There were problems of peripherality, there were
problems of economical development. There were problems of
the misfortune to be beside a neighbour that was very
powerful. Strategically, we are very important to the defence of
that particular island, so geography was something that over-
determined our history and over-determined our economics.
What happened in the 1980s, with the investment in the
digitalisation of the telecommunications network, was that we
got the development of what we call the network-based or
reticular economy where you can provide services and goods
through the information and telecommunications network
rather than relying on physical methods of transportation or
communication. So we got the emergence of the International
Financial Services Centre, we got the growth in call centres,
telesales and telemarketing.

This is why in 2003 Ireland emerges in the AT Kearney and
Foreign Policy Survey as the most globalised country out of sixty-
two states that were chosen for the survey. What do they mean by
the most globalised country? What they are looking at is the

degree of integration of each nation state into the world's political and economic system. How do they rank this? They look at international trade. They look at multinational investment. They look at telephone call volumes. For all these things to happen to the extent that they did is very much dependent on the shift to the informatics and telecommunications network-based economy. In other words, we had the shift from geo-politics to chrono-politics. In this context, the competitive advantage of small nations is to take the waiting out of wanting. In other words, it is about how quickly you can deliver the services. This has had all kinds of consequences for Irish life. Consequences that don't often get talked about.

One of the consequences is what I would call the 'chrono-stratification' of Irish life. There has been a lot written about how our cities and towns have been spatially divided by a kind of social apartheid. The way in which certain social classes are living in certain parts of the cities and towns. The way we see the emergence of gated communities, intercom systems and so on in Ireland. This is the spatial distribution of wealth in Ireland. What is less talked about is the kind of stratification in Irish society on the basis of your access to rapid or accelerated time. In other words, we have one section of the society that is part of the global, nomadic elite, which is circling the globe endlessly. And there are other groups in our society – the poor, the unemployed, the sick, the rural poor in particular – who have no access to public transport. In fact, as one elderly woman in north Mayo said about her free travel pass, it was like being given a saddle without a horse, because there was no public transport system to speak of in north Mayo. This kind of chrono-stratification of the society is a very real one and one that is intensifying as the notion of mobility quickness, acceleration, becomes a highly prized status symbol in the society itself. What we have lived through in the last ten years is a society that is very much part of the traditional dream of modernisation, which is a dream of acceleration. This includes everything from physical, infrastructural developments, the building of roads, the building of bridges, runways and so on, to the present trust to provide broadband capacity throughout the island.

This, if you like, is a version of emancipation, what one thinker, Paul Virilio, called 'dromophilia' – '*dromos*', the Greek word for 'speed' and '*philos*', the Greek word for love – the love of speed, the notion of speed and acceleration as a true form of emancipation or liberation for society. This happens at two levels, at a European level and at national level. At European level, it is the positive notion of Europe. It is Europe as a kind of kinetic utopia where it is no longer armies that are on the move, but goods, services and, to a lesser extent, people. So on the one hand you have the immobility of nationalist Europe, which is characterised by the First World War. It is characterised by attrition. It is characterised by people who were there in the trenches, who were immobilised by the orthodoxy of nationalist conviction. This is contrasted with the great mobility, the enhanced mobility of post-nationalist Europe, whose most eloquent symbol is Ryanair and Michael O'Leary. Revolution and emancipation are a kind of acceleration of everything. This is most beautifully expressed by the most unlikely of people; the Formula One correspondent of the *Irish Times*, Justin Hynes, in a piece on the introduction of the driving licence points system (2 November 2002), said the following:

> I am not a fool. Yet I am being treated like one by a nanny State that wants to stop us smoking, drinking and driving and live docile, sheep-like lives of expressionless homogeneity, preferably on a bus.

So you see Hynes is making an equation between the notion of individual emancipation, modernisation and the idea of the speed. He says that the points system will remove from our grasp 'one of the great pleasures of modern existence – the ability to control your own destiny at the controls of a machine of wonderful liberation', which is rather a grand way of describing getting into a Toyota Corolla and moving into gear. What interests me is that if you actually look at the last two or three years, at a number of demonstrations in the city, the way in which the State has reacted shows the extent to which it is committed at a very profound level to this notion of dromophilia as emancipation. During the farmers' demonstration in 1998 one particular political representative suggested that farmers not march through the city because they were going to interfere with commuters, that they should, in fact, stay in the Phoenix Park. You could not have farmers, who were depicted as the slow-moving agents of the population, impeding fast-moving commuters. In 2001 there was a cyclist action group demonstration in Westmoreland Street and it was broken up in an extremely brutal fashion by the Gardaí. At the anti-globalisation protest in 2002 in College Green, the reason for the intervention, which again was heavy-handed, was the claim that the demonstrators were interfering with the traffic. So, in fact, what you had there is a kind of battle over time zones. One group, the agents of the State, reclaiming the streets for the private car and the other group reclaiming it for the pedestrians.

But of course, the flip side of this dromophilia is what is called 'dromophobia' – the fear of speed. This is the kind of down side that we have been experiencing over the last decade as well. The first is the myth of frictionless circulation, that if we build more roads, if you add to the infrastructure of the cars, you will be able to move quicker and quicker with less and less difficulty. Of course, what we see is increasing congestion – the more roads we build, the more cars there are to fill them and the more likely it is that we are going to get traffic jams. The introduction of the points system, which specifically targeted the whole area of speeding is very much a reaction of society at some level, which is to deal with the consequences of dromophilia – dromophilia gone mad. More particularly it seems to me there are consequences in two areas that I want to dwell on more in a little more detail – the workplace and the media.

The Norwegian sociologist Thomas Hyland Eriksen talks about what he calls the 'tyranny of the moment'. What he means by this is, if you have a society, a global economy, of which we are an integral part, which works in real time, the different activities of production and consumption are taking place in real time and planetary scale. That has immediate consequences for the way in which people experience time. Dr Miriam Moore, in her report on *Wellbeing and Stress in the Workplace*, which was produced by the Céifin Institute, found that over 50 per cent of the respondents in her survey complained about being caught up in the rat race. One third of the respondents said that they were chronically tired most of the time. If you reflect back on the last decade, you will find that you have spent more and more time doing one major thing and that is processing or dealing with information. If you think of the increase in telephone calls, fax messages, emails, the amount of time you spend going to meetings, the amount of time you spend reading minutes, the time you spend writing minutes, the time you spend filing minutes – all these information processing activities are taking up more and more of our time. But the crucial thing about information processing activities, of course, is the speed at which they are taking place. It might take you a week to reply to a letter, but a day to reply to a fax. In the case of an email message, if the reply doesn't come back within the half hour, you get another saying, 'Are you still there? Are you sick? Are you still with us?' So it is the actual time of response that is radically shortened.

If you think of the mobile phone, one of the things about it is that it fills in the gaps in our lives. In other words, those moments when we are on our way from point A to B, when we are standing at the bus stop. When we are sitting on the beach.

These gaps, if you like, can be filled by the mobile phone. The mobile phone is a symbol of the way in which human time, which in the average human day is a fixed span of human time, comes under increasing pressure. Some people sleep more or less than others. There are even accelerated waking techniques where you can sleep less and less, but most people tend to sleep an average amount of time. The problem is that in a fixed span of time, we are trying to fit in more and more. What you get is information overload. The deadline frenzy.

The *New York Times* on a Saturday has as much information in it as an educated French person in the eighteenth century would absorb in an entire lifetime. Ignacio Ramonet who has studied this question of the increase in information, estimates that in the last twenty years in the average western society, the amount of information we have had to absorb has increased by a factor of three hundred. Now the thing is, the length of day for people living in an average western society has not increased by three hundred times. We still have our twenty-four hour day, twelve hours of which are waking hours. So what Eriksen says is that we are arriving at a situation which I think is characteristic of many areas of contemporary Irish life. He says that everything becomes a hysterical series of saturated moments without a before and after, a here and there, to separate them. Indeed, even the here and now is threatened because the next moment comes so quickly that it becomes so difficult to live in the present. The result of that is that it becomes increasingly difficult to think about the future, and indeed, it becomes increasingly difficult to make sense of the present. In talking to people over the last while, one of the things that struck me that people are under so much pressure very often, that they literally do not have time to take stock or try to make sense of what is happening to them. At some level there is a chrono-sickness in the society, which is one of the things we have to think about in terms of change.

One of the areas where it seems to me the notion of acceleration has really become very visible and audible is the area of the media, both the print media and the broadcast media. One of the difficulties when you want to disagree with someone is that it takes time. It takes even more time when you want to disagree with someone who is uttering a platitude, a piece of what is seen as common sense, a kind of conventional way of thinking about things, because very often if you want to disagree with the platitudes, the conventional, you have to go back to basics. That takes time, and then you have to advance, put forward unusual ideas, which take time to explain. The problem is that time is precisely the commodity that is becoming scarcer and scarcer so that what you end up with very often is the kind of sedentary economy of binary sound bites. So it is things like, 'Are you for terrorism or are you against terrorism? Please answer the question. Are you for public spending cuts or recklessness with the public finances? Please answer this question in thirty seconds.' So what it privileges is the emergence of what the French sociologist Pierre Bourdieu calls 'le fast thinker', somebody whose eye is not so much on the truth as on the clock, who tends to specialise in the zap, the killer statistic, that mixture of personal anecdote and polemical affirmation, which means that argument and reflection get evacuated. So very often the reaction of listeners is that they feel angry, baffled, but not very enlightened, and what very often tends to happen, is that people get confirmed in the prejudices they started off with in the first place.

The second aspect of the effects or the impact of this chrono-politicisation of acceleration on the media is fundamental contradiction in society over the last decade between the fact that more and more people in Ireland have had access to formal education, but the media have less and less to offer them. At the same time that we have a society that has become more and more educated, there are fewer and fewer media outlets for the discussion and thoughtful explanation of ideas. In other words, the more we talk about an information society in Ireland, the more we talk about a knowledge society in Ireland, the more the actual infrastructure for the dissemination of thought, of reflection and ideas is constantly shrinking. If you look at the demise of *Hibernia*, look at the demise of *Magill*, look at the demise of *In Dublin*, look at the demise of *The Crane Bag*. If you think of the number of broadcasters in the various radio and television stations who have a particular, specific interest in cultural and intellectual programming, that number is diminishing all the time. So the more we are talking about this knowledge or information society it seems to me the less and less we are doing in the construction of a public sphere that will make that a very genuine reality because if you want to turn information into knowledge, you need time to reflect on this information. You need time to digest it so it does become a form of knowledge. But one of the paradoxes of the last decade is that we are getting more and more information, but we are getting correspondingly less and less meaning.

One of the departments in my own faculty in Dublin City University is called the School of Communications. This was a word that Dean Swift held in such horror that when a friend of his uttered it in his presence, Swift threw a bowl of pears at him. He thought the word was an abomination in the English language. Of course, communication is something that is talked about constantly in terms of a globalised Irish society. But if we are talking about communication we must make a fundamental distinction between what I would call 'transmission' and what we call 'communication'. 'Communication', for me, is the communication or the transport of information across space in the same historical period, sending information from point A to B in the same real time. 'Transmission', on the other hand, is the sending, the communication of information across time, across different historical periods. In order for transmission to happen you need two things. You need a medium, something that actually carries this information across time; this could be stone from the Ogham inscriptions; it could be paper, vellum, parchment, the invention of the printing press or, more recently, the magnetic disk. We also need what is called a social vector. Some kind of body that is responsible for this process of transmission. This needs to be an organised body, in other words, if individual members of this die, the body as a whole will survive through time, so this can be a school, a university, a trade union, a solidarity action group. It can be a Church, a nation State, it can, indeed, be a family. There is one version of Irish modernisation which would say that Ireland was a spectacular victim of transmission. In other words, that what Irish society for many decades was primarily concerned with was the question of transmission. At a State level, this was the transmission of a nationalist orthodoxy, a particular view of the genesis, origins and values of the Irish State, politically and in terms of the majority Church, the notion of a specific set of beliefs or dogmas that were transmitted by the Church. In the reaction against that, in the last ten or fifteen years, we have had the kind of transition from the transmissive society to the communicative society. We have a society linked up with communicative euphoria, this map of global connectedness, of which Ireland is one of the important nodes. In this vision, transmission gets a very bad press. Transmission is a bit like the *Seanfhear Liath*, the Old Grey Man, in *An Béal Bocht* by Myles Na gCopaleen, with his feet in the ashes, muttering away about the relics of old decency, the good old days and so on. But it is difficult to see how a society can endure, indeed, how this society will endure, if we do not have some kind of ethics of transmission. At one stage in Irish life, one could say that Ireland was transmissive society obsessed with ends, the end being Ireland's freedom or its place among the nations, or the fate of our souls. If there is a shift from a transmissive to a communicative society, obsessed not so much with ends as with means – so the whole emphasis on national competitiveness, broadband coverage, the extent of government borrowing and so on – does that mean that we now live in an Ireland that is post-revolutionary, communicative, and whose central goal in its values system is that of perpetual self-enrichment?

Another paradox of the last decade is that while we move towards a more deregulated economy, we now live in an ever more regulated civil society, with an unprecedented extension of Garda powers, with particular social classes finding themselves very much the victims of the prison system, and a huge increase in litigation over the past decade. In other words, in the absence of shared values and common ends, are external coercion and the administrations of the courts the only grounds we have for living together in social cohesion? As I said, it seems to me that it is not a fact that is often acknowledged that we have lived through a revolution. It is a revolution that has been animated by two things: market fundamentalism and social liberalism. It is a revolution that is particularly confusing for a lot of people because it is a revolution that is both reactionary and progressive at the same time. One of the things it has shown is that change is possible. Change has happened on a spectacular scale in the last decade. The challenge, of course, is for us to change that change and to change it in a way that means we have an Ireland that serves the ends of the many rather than the means of the few.

It seems to me that there are three ways in which we can address the issue of change and try to do something practical about it. The first is what I would call the recognition of social time. Very often when we think of development and progress, we think of it in terms of what I would call technical time. In other words, that you go from the horse to the car to the airliner. There is a sort of linear progression from one to the other. But societies do not just work in technical time, they also work in social time. What some people refer to as the jogging effect. One of the things that was argued when motor cars first appeared and then became increasingly popular, was that our legs would gradually wither away, that we would have these weak, limp appendages, but they would be no use. We would just have these torsos sitting in cars, which would carry us around the place. But what has happened is not extinction. It is exhaustion. Look at the number of people who are running, jogging, or walking through our cities and towns. More and more of them. Look at the number of people taking part in the Dublin City Marathon and others. Societies do not in their social and cultural practices go forward in that kind of linear progressive way. What happens is that they often loop backwards to things that were considered to be obsolete, but then enjoyed a new life. One of the things we can do is to look at elements of the Irish past and see what elements are potentially progressive. One of them is a standard element of Tudor propaganda from the sixteenth century, that the Irish poets were obsessed with genealogy – with *ginealach* – that they were forever reciting these great long genealogical lists, which was seen as their cultural and social retardation. You could look at something like this notion of genealogy as something that could be quite subversive. Because there is hardly a family in Ireland that has not had people who have gone and lived elsewhere, who have emigrated to other countries. By making school children, for example, aware of this, then it is possible to empathise in a very real and immediate way with the experiences and plight of people coming to live in Ireland, whether they be economic or political migrants.

Secondly, I think we need a new form of political kinetics. What I mean by that is when people traditionally think of revolution, whether they be liberals or Marxists, they see it in terms of the acceleration of the productive process. That if we do things faster and faster and more efficiently that this is going to be the great emancipation. But maybe what we need is not so much a revolution of acceleration, but a revolution of deceleration, the idea that *Festina Lente*, make haste slowly, that less is more. For example, in Italy, along with the slow food movement, there is the slow town movement where cars are banned from the town centres, shops close at particular times, agreed on with the people in the towns, so the producers and consumers act together on this one. We could have what is called the decelerated architecture movement where there are parts of the building out of the range of the mobile phone. Nobody can contact you in that space. There are no computer terminals. These would be the decelerated spaces in the building, whereas more and more architecture, is designed for a politics of acceleration.

Thirdly, there is what has been called the diversity dividend. Over 250,000 people in the last six years came from abroad to live in Ireland. This should be seen as a source of enrichment, but it should properly be seen as a source of enrichment in a way that respects the otherness of others. One of the dangerous things is to come up with a kind of easy assumption that everybody should be just like us or everybody else is just like us. This is in fact, one of the most damaging ways of refusing another person's integrity or respect, because if you do that the other person just becomes an enlarged projection of yourself. I am working with some colleagues in my own faculty on a planned project called 'Babel Átha Cliath'. This is a project for schools in the North Dublin area, where pilot classes or groups are chosen and introduced to Mandarin Chinese, Urdu, Russian and Romanian, which are the languages spoken by a lot of people living in the north Dublin area. So the idea is that children are investing time in this activity and realising that the Russian speakers, the Romanian speakers, the Urdu speakers have this extraordinary linguistic and cultural knowledge. But it is something that takes time. A lot has changed in the last decade. As I speak things are still changing, but I think it is up to all of us here, both today and tomorrow to take up this gauntlet and to make sure the revolution serves the ends of the many rather than the means of a minority elite in society.

GLOBAL CHANGE
MAKING THE WORLD A HOME FOR ALL

H.E. Melanie Verwoerd

While working on my speech in the last few days, I was reminded of the series of books that our eleven-year-old son is busy reading. It is called 'A Series of Unfortunate Events'. I suddenly felt that I have to put a warning at the beginning of this talk as the author Lemony Snicket does in this series. He starts all his books with the following rather unusual introduction: 'If you are interested in stories with happy endings, you would be better off reading some other book. In this book, not only is there no happy ending, there is no happy beginning and very few happy things in the middle.' I trust that my talk to you today will not be quite as grim and dark as the Snicket introduction suggests, because in my heart I am an optimist, even though I do sometimes associate with the EU Commissioner for the Environment who described herself as 'a despairing optimist'.

Please know also that when I share some of my ideas, frustrations and sometimes anger with you, I do so, not with a sense of moral superiority, but as a person who stands with one foot in the so called developed world and one foot in the developing world. As a white person who grew up during apartheid years in one of the worst systems of human oppression, I, like most other white South Africans, lived a completely secluded life and rarely made contact with people of other races, who were suffering so bitterly. I received a totally western education and was taught western literature, religion and art. Through a series of events I found myself questioning all the values and the ideology that were fed to us and eventually through a long painful journey found myself rejecting much of what I was taught. I found myself using my energy to learn from and work with those that were oppressed. So I became part of a process of breaking down the apartheid regime and later, as a member of parliament for the ANC, rebuilding a democratic, multicultural country – certainly one of the most exciting events of the twentieth century.

Today, I know that even though much of my head will remain filled with western thought patterns and knowledge, my soul and my heart are in Africa and I proclaim proudly as our president did at the adoption of our new constitution: 'I am an African.'

So when I speak to you today I do so as someone who has really seen and felt some of the frustration of those who have, through a stroke of history, been born into a place, a global system and a time where they are to a large degree rendered powerless by so many circumstances outside their control. Nothing illustrates this tragic situation better than an experience my staff and I had recently. Earlier this year we received a call to the embassy from a hospital in Dublin. They wanted us to visit a South African patient, Linda. Some of my staff went immediately and this became a journey that touched many of us in the embassy profoundly. The woman we went to visit was an asylum seeker from South Africa. She lived with her family in a squatter camp outside Johannesburg and from what we could establish later was desperately poor. Like many others she had heard stories of a better life in Europe – confirmed by the daily bombardment of television images of the nice life people in Europe and the West have. So she came to Ireland and applied for asylum, hoping that she would get permanent status once she had given birth to her little daughter. She gave birth shortly after arriving in Ireland and named her little girl Mary. Then things started going wrong. I do not know whether Linda was aware that she had Aids, but through a string of unfortunate events she became extremely ill. When we went to see her she was on a life support system. She died a few days later. Nobody came to visit, nobody came to ask where she was and it was only through the extraordinary care of her doctor that we could get into her mobile phone to find some numbers to try and trace her family.

The real tragedy is, of course, her little daughter, Mary. She was and remains alone in a foreign country, also sick with this devastating virus that hit Sub-Saharan Africa so hard. Her dad is also an asylum seeker – in England – and could not even travel to see her. There are so many layers to this story that I could speak for another hour just on this, but I can tell you that the day that Linda was cremated (her parents could not afford to bring her body home) – alone with just some of the embassy staff present, with a lonely South African beaded flag on her coffin, with her tiny baby somewhere in the care of the Irish state – I knew that their story represented so much of what is not well in this world. On Mary's little shoulders rested so many of the burdens that have made this globe such an unwelcoming place for so many (in fact two-thirds) of her sons and daughters.

During these days I was often reminded of the words of the Nobel laureate and former president of the ANC Albert Luthuli, when he remarked in the early 1960s:

> The task is not finished. South Africa is not yet a home for all her sons and daughters. Such a home we wish to ensure. From the beginning our history has been one of ascending unities, the breaking of tribal, racial and credal barriers. There remains before us the building of a new

land, a home for men who are black, white, brown, from the ruins of the old narrow groups.

It seems to me that this challenge of Luthuli in the 1960s to South Africa remains the challenge for us all today and it seems to me that this is what we are talking about today at this conference – to create a world where all her citizens can feel at home.

The problem is that none of us can deny that all is not well in this global village. In fact, we are increasingly faced with a world where there are deeply troubling signs that we are often NOT able to break through 'tribal, racial and credal barriers' and where despite a tremendous increase in wealth and affluence in some parts, more and more people are faced with desperate and dehumanising poverty – making them feel like foreigners in this global village.

For example, out of its 6 billion inhabitants, 1.2 billion go hungry every day, 1.2 billion lack access to clean water, nearly one billion adults are illiterate. On the other hand, according to a recent Worldwatch Report, the number of people in the world who are overweight and over-nourished also now measures around 1.2 billion. Is it not shocking that we face one news article after the other about obesity being the new disease in the developed world, while elsewhere 1.2 billion people are always hungry? Another shocking statistic is that if people in the United States would reduce their meat consumption by 10 per cent, the saving in grain needed to feed the cattle would be enough to feed the chronically hungry people in the world. Or closer to home: did you know that each year the EU spends more than €300 million on agricultural subsidies and only €50 million on aid?

These are only a few statistics and it is easy to become numbed by statistics. However, they are not cold numbers when you come from a country and continent where we see the effects of global policies, or when you look in the eyes of a little baby like Mary. It cannot leave you untouched when you sit amongst Aids infected babies in Nazareth House in Cape Town, like I recently did, and the Irish nuns tell you how they have discovered that the little ones seem to make silent agreements that they will die together – so that when one dies the friends almost always die shortly afterwards. In fact it leaves me not only with a deep sense of pain and failure, but also with a blind anger since it would have cost the world around three Euro per person (the price of a Big Mac at McDonalds) to give them the medication that would have prevented the transmission of this deadly disease. Or when I looked through the Christmas wishes that little children submitted to a foundation in South Africa and so many cards ask only for 'new underwear, or school books for next year, or a football for my brother, or food to have a Christmas lunch'.

Surely when we see and hear this we must in the words of Irish poet Kinsella be 'hurt into action'.

So how do we then answer this call for action? There is of course the global and the individual perspective. But in both cases it seems to me that the process starts with awareness – with listening. But listening is often not enough: we must also truly hear. In our world today we know more than ever before about what is going on – we know about the poverty, the violence. None of us can claim ignorance. But I believe that through maybe a way of self-protection or feelings of helplessness, we have succeeded in listening to these things without really hearing.

To start hearing, to listen deeply, we have to look each other in the eyes and understand this collective responsibility that we hold towards each other. To understand that we are responsible not only for ourselves or our families or even our society, but that we share a collective responsibility towards all those we share this earth with.

Once we have come to hear the pain we have to understand that the inequality and pain does not come about in a vacuum, but is created amongst others by current global systems and our life-styles in the 'one-thirds world'. Clearly this means that at a national, international, and also at an individual level we need real change.

At an international level it clearly requires us to seriously re-think the global order and specifically the global economic order that we live in. Of course it is true that many developing nations still require and will continue to require Development Aid. On a personal level it seems crucial that all continue with their contributions to very worthy aid organisations. But it is generally understood that for real development to take place, for us to create a truly just global order, something far more fundamental has to happen.

This includes a restructuring of international bodies, such as the UN and WTO in order for the developing, or two-thirds, world to have their rightful say. It also involves ensuring greater access to markets in the rich world, and in particularly a re-look at international agricultural policies. In some cases it also requires a levelling of the playing field by a careful writing off of debt.

I so often hear people say that firstly they have no responsibility towards development issues, since they have nothing to do with the causes and secondly that even if they do there is nothing they can do to make a difference. This is rather similar to what we saw in South Africa post-1994. Since the democratic elections the previously advantaged increasingly privatised their citizenship. You constantly heard and still hear privileged people say: let us now forgive and forget, let us get on with life. The problem with this attitude was beautifully illustrated by a parable told by Rev. Mpambani at the hearings of the Truth and Reconciliation Commission:

> There were two boys – let us call them Tom and Peter. One day Tom stole Peter's bicycle. But after a while Tom felt bad and went back to Peter. He said: 'Listen Peter, I stole your bicycle. I am sorry. Please forgive me.' 'But

what about my bicycle?', asked Peter. To which Tom replied: 'Well, I am not talking about your bicycle now, I am talking about forgiveness.'

This is of course the problem. Until the proverbial bicycle has been returned, we will not be able to say that we have built a country where all her sons and daughters are truly at home or a truly just society. Of course people do not like to be reminded of collective responsibilities and would deny that they had anything to do with the previous system and, therefore, its legacy. Instead we are seeing more and more walls going up (literally and metaphorically). People are privatising their citizenship – and daily living becomes a never-ending rush or drive to be able to maintain this privacy through material wealth.

Having spent more than two years in Ireland it seems that increasing concerns are being raised about this gradual loss of community. But it seems that this tendency to privatise citizenship is also mirrored in our global citizenship and a lack of consciousness about how our lives directly influence those of others – and not always for the better. In South Africa, whites gained education and wealth not in a neutral environment, but in an environment that gave them the wealth and education at the expense of others. Equally the developed world has the wealth and resources not because the developing world is hopeless or stupid, but because of global systems that mostly benefit the developed world.

So, can the individual in Ireland or anywhere else make a difference? Of course! How we shop, how we do business, where we choose to invest our money, where and how we have our holidays, how we vote, the questions we raise in the media and the extent to which we get involved can make a REAL difference.

I think if there is one thing that globalisation has taught us or should teach us, it is that we are all linked, that we are all part of the global village, where what we do in one part affects the other part, which in turn affects us again. In Africa there is the extraordinary philosophy of Ubuntu, which can be summed in the expression 'umuntu ngumuntu ngbantu' – 'people are people through other people'. It seems to me that we all have to learn to live with a deeper awareness of our fundamental connectedness as fellow citizens on our small, fragile planet.

With regards to the fragility of our shared global home I briefly want to point to a further level of privatisation, which urgently needs to be countered. This level of privatisation involves the natural world. Fundamentally it seems that the human race is increasingly claiming its right to take what we want (and not necessarily need) with very little regard for the effect this taking is having on the natural world and the environment. Daniel Quinn makes the distinction between takers and leavers; between those who take at all costs and those who take, but only to the extent that they can leave things as they were. It is extraordinary to remember that all we need – air, water, sustenance and shelter – is given to us in the natural world for free. And yet through our greediness we are destroying these resources at a rate that could finally lead to our own extinction. It seems to me that unless we can see ourselves as not only part of the human global order, but also responsible role players in the natural global environment, that we will eventually privatise ourselves into extinction.

I said in the beginning that I am an optimist. So do I believe things can change? Yes, I do. Almost ten years ago on 25 April 1994, I went to bed at four in the morning not knowing whether we would have a country left twenty-four hours later. I had slept for an hour when I got a call from one of my friends in the ANC election team, who urged me to come to the township (black area) immediately. I drove apprehensively, expecting the worst. As I came closer to the township, I could not believe my eyes. It was pouring with rain, pitch dark and freezing, but as far as I could see people were standing in the rain patiently waiting for the polling booths to open three hours later. Even though we reassured them that there were two days to vote and that we would pick them up later, nobody would move. There were babies with little hoods made of plastic shopping bags on the backs of their mothers, the elderly with walking sticks and the disabled in wheelbarrows, but nothing, nothing would get them to move and run the risk of missing the chance to vote for the first time. Two weeks later I stood with a jubilant crowd at Nelson Mandela's inauguration and watched how young white soldiers flew past in fighter jets and saluted their new president.

Of course change is possible. It is not easy, but it is possible. It is not only possible; it is our moral responsibility.

A few comments have been made about age – or the lack of it in my case! So it seems appropriate to quote Yeats when he says in 'Sailing to Byzantium', 'That is no country for old men'. Our President Thabo Mbeki said the following in relation to this quote 'to entertain a vision (where all is free from poverty, ignorance and human degradation), one should be young, not necessarily in years, but young in one's ability to break with the past, in one's capacity to remove from oneself the shackles of old thinking, allowing oneself to be inspired by the notion, that where there is no vision, people perish'.

These reflections on our shared moral responsibility to create a global home for all her sons and daughters bring me, in conclusion, to the inspiring words quoted by Nelson Mandela at his presidential inauguration in 1994:

> Our deepest fear is not that we are inadequate. Our deepest fear is that we are powerful beyond measure. It is our light, not our darkness that most frightens us. We ask ourselves 'Who am I to be brilliant. Gorgeous, talented, fabulous?' Actually who are you not to be? There's nothing enlightened about shrinking so that other people won't feel insecure around you. We were all meant to

shine as children do. It is not just in some of us; it's in everyone. And as we let our light shine we unconsciously give other people permission to do the same. As we are liberated from our own fear, our presence automatically liberates others.

'THEY'RE A FINE PAIR OF SHOES YOU HAVE DOCTOR'
— THE NATURE OF CARING

Sinéad Donnelly

As a doctor working in palliative medicine, looking after people who are dying in hospice care, changes happen very quickly, acutely and intensely. The team of carers must pay great attention to the detail of care both for the person who is very ill and dying and to their family and friends. In a way, it is like helping to prepare a beautiful manuscript; the manuscript of the person's life as it comes to a close. The work that we do in palliative care is intense, labour-intensive, and could be viewed by other health practitioners as attending to unnecessary detail. However, I feel that we are, in fact, helping to prepare a script of a person's life at a critical time.

I accompany people who are preparing to die. These people usually have advanced cancer or perhaps motor neuron disease and the fact of having such a disease creates a climate of huge potential change on a daily basis, if not hour by hour, for the individual and their family. Part of my job is to facilitate quality of life in the midst of this change, which may even be chaotic, and the question is 'How can I be present in a professional manner in the midst of such rapid change?'

Those doctors who work in palliative medicine as I do, or in palliative care, are interested in a holistic way in the individual who is suffering. I am interested not only in their physical wellbeing, but in all the other components that create suffering, emotional, social, spiritual.

As a doctor working in the twenty-first century I believe that I can learn a lot from looking to the past, for example, the tradition and practice surrounding death and dying in Ireland. I remember seeing some wonderful photographs of a funeral on one of the Aran Islands. The procession was so dignified and respectful. For me, it said a lot about the mystery of death, its impact on the community and how the community can deal with its grief.

There is a phrase in the Irish language – '*Ó ta nádúr aige*' – when they are describing someone – 'Oh, he's got nature, there's nature in him.' '*Nádúr*' directly translated means 'nature', but in Irish it also reflects philosophy. How does one have 'nature' in one? It is this 'nature' that people who are ill or who are vulnerable need most from the professional. There is another Irish word particularly used in the west of Scotland – '*caochail*'– and it refers to the death of people as distinct from the death of animals. Here people refer to death as a change – a transmutation – a change in substance. The language we use reflects our attitudes to change, to humanity, to life and to death. In caring for people who are dying now, I believe I can learn a lot from the philosophy of Irish people in the past.

How can I capture the closeness to the spirit world, the sense of community, the acceptance of mystery that was part of our attitude to dying and death in the past? How can I take elements, the essence of that, and bring it into the present to create change and improve standards of care? There must be a way that I can capture the richness of the past, moving it into the present, informing the present and improving care.

I want to tell you three stories of people whose lives underwent change – dramatic change – and in which palliative care, the hospice team, were involved.

I first met Liam Hughes, sixty-two years of age from County Limerick, in April 2002. He was told that he had partial blockage of the bowel, which was subsequently found to be due to cancer.

On a Monday morning I met Mr Hughes in the Mid Western Regional Hospital and I remember the occasion vividly. Mr Hughes had a bed in an open male surgical ward. When I and the Palliative Care nurse went to the ward to visit him his bed was empty. We eventually figured out that he was in the bathroom. He declined to emerge so we said we would come back later. On the third occasion in attempting to meet him I actually knocked on the toilet door. The door opened slightly and two large eyes were visible surrounded by shaving cream. We talked through the slightly opened door to the man with big eyes. He didn't want to meet the doctor. Eventually we walked together to his bed and tried to discuss what was troubling him. He had lived all his life as a single man, alone. He seemed frightened and he admitted to pain in his tummy.

He was convinced by the Palliative Care nurse to come to the Hospice Unit to recover from his recent surgery. He understood that his bowel was stuck and twisted and he hoped to gain strength and eventually go home. Throughout his stay of several weeks he was often quite distressed. When there was a foul-smelling discharge from the wound he believed it was because I had examined his stomach and caused it. Often he was angry with the number of tablets that he had to take, but he didn't want us to change them at all. His aim was to gain weight and he was distressed when after two weeks he said – 'Why am I here? I haven't put on any weight.' But later he was able to say – 'What's the point of dying in comfort, I'm better off in the fresh air at home. ' Eventually, he did gain weight and was delighted. He understood that the doctors and nurses would continue to care for him and do the best for him and he said – 'You can do no more, this is the right place for me.'

However, the following week he was in a poor mood and very irritable because he was worried about the sheep at home in County Limerick – that they were scattered and possibly stolen. So he went home for a few days and came back upset because the fire hadn't been lit for months and it was very cold in the house. He wanted the Health Board to provide a Stanley range and not electric heaters because that would be too expensive for him. Later he was very keen to bring his red truck to the Hospice and to commute from home, but to sleep in the Hospice. Once he came back from a outing at home with a dog bite, which he wouldn't allow us to treat.

Finally he was discharged home for five months, but came in again and died in the Unit.

I remember caring for Mr Hughes in the final few weeks of his life. I was amazed at the change in personality. A man who used four-letter words and protected himself defensively against us was now open to all help.

A week before he died I had been concerned about the progressive curving in his back with the result that when he actually stood up he was looking at the floor all the time. His head was facing the floor. He had difficulty eating his bowl of porridge in the morning because he actually had to stand rather than sit in order to get the spoon to his mouth to be able to swallow it. A diagnosis of arthritis had been made and that was probably the cause of the curvature. It was his eyes that I had first seen when I met him through the toilet door. Now his eyes were disappearing from my view as his neck became more curved.

Each morning we visited him in his room and one morning as he stood and I sat so that we could actually see each other in some way, he said – in the midst of his questions about the progressive nature of his cancer – 'They're a fine pair of shoes you have, Doctor.' It was amusing in that his main view was now of the floor and all he could see of interest at the time were my feet. The phrase really was most poignant in view of the blossoming of his personality that had occurred within this space of care.

The world of palliative medicine is all about change. In the past it was seen as a place to die. Now it is seen as a place of holistic care where attention is paid to all the dimensions of a person as a human being.

As I attend in my humanity to someone who is ill and possibly dying, in the same way I must approach those with whom I work. They will learn to care for those who are ill according to how they are treated by their colleagues. I remember when I went to work in a hospice in Scotland, I was taken aback that my first duty was to go into a cold storage area in the morning, accompanied by a porter, and sign off in the book that the bodies as shown here were dead. That is how my work in a Hospice began each morning. That is not what I would ask of doctors in training. For a young doctor to arrive and to have to look after people who will die – as one young doctor described recently, working in the hospice was initially like a conveyor belt of death – I must attend to their well-being and, via my approach to those who are dying and those who are ill, they will learn how to practise a medicine of healing and caring.

The second story is about Annie Murphy, a fifty-five-year-old lady from the outskirts of Limerick city. She was married to Tony and they had four children aged from fifteen to twenty-two years of age. I met Mrs Murphy in the Mid Western Regional Hospital. I was struck by her quietness and the burden of her anxiety and sorrow. Mrs Murphy had had breast carcinoma since October 2002. She had had surgery and chemotherapy, but the cancer had spread to her bones causing a rise of calcium in her body, which was causing her to be nauseated.

She agreed to come to the Palliative Care Unit to help control the nausea, but she wanted to persist with any further chemotherapy. It was clear that her husband was distraught, crying frequently. He appeared to have little in the way of support system and wanted to protect his children. During her stay Mrs Murphy's blood count was dropping and her calcium remained very high, causing her to be still sick and vomiting. She tried to go home for a few hours on several occasions, but was too sick. There were family meetings involving Mrs

Murphy, her husband and the children as well as the professional team. The aim was to gently prepare them for what was inevitable, which was that Mrs Murphy's prognosis was very poor and that her death was imminent, although the family and she did not seem to grasp that completely.

I remember a weekend when her gums began to bleed and we gave her a special type of blood and special medication. As I stood there knowing the significance of the bleeding gums, and feeling that she didn't know that significance, I felt very inadequate as if I was supposed to be God because I understood what this meant and she was physically feeling it, but didn't understand the significance. I wrote at the time:

> I stick to the window pane of death like a wet blown autumn leaf,
> I hear the tap of nail wood hammered,
> blood clot palms plead upturned and stigmatised,
> she sits with fearful eyes and bleeding gums alert to this fading life.
> How dare I stand before her silent,
> knowing that she bleeds into her death stretch.
> How barbaric to calmly witness another mortal queue.

I suppose in writing this I was trying to deal with my own feelings about death.

That evening I visited Mrs Murphy. Her gums were bleeding and she was frightened. I stood beside her and tried to explain how the transfusion of platelets would protect her. The following day was Palm Sunday and she said, 'I will die in a few days.' She realised she was getting weaker. The Sunday leaflet of the Passion was on her bed with a branch of palm. That day I also met her husband Tony. We sat together on a wooden bench in the unit and he said, 'I must protect them, my son is doing exams. No matter what I do it will be wrong. If I don't send him to the exams he'll have to repeat, if I send him to exams and something happens to his mother here, that will be the wrong thing. They all think I know at home... I know nothing.' He started to cry, and he was embarrassed to be crying in front of a woman. And then he recounted the misfortunes of the year – problems with a heifer, then Annie with her first operation, then problems with the fridge, the washing machine, the cooker, they all broke down. All small misfortunes, but this year, this is trouble. He said, 'Annie told me I'd be alright, but I don't know.'

Mrs Murphy died a week later.

In dealing with all of this change, how do I and how do the professionals remain steady? I am drawn more and more to a greater creativity, both in the work I do and in expression outside of work. I have been struck by the power of silence and I like to begin the day with the team with a moment of quiet before we discuss how the sick people have been overnight. And out of this silence and need to be more creative, I approach the teaching of young doctors differently in that we try to include the humanities and exploration of art as part of the teaching session each week. I like to use photographs, film and video, subsequently making a documentary as a way of teaching and explaining what we try to do. I am more and more drawn towards qualitative research in the sense of exploring people's stories and letting their voices speak, because at the end on a Friday or on a weekend it does seem like too much death and the journey that I take and that we take as a team can seem excessively burdened. And each day I'm reminded of my own mortality; we are all targeted to die.

The final story is of a lady whose family's life changed and whose personality affected all the team and somehow changed me.

Kristen was diagnosed with breast cancer in August 2002. She declined all the regular forms of treatment and went for alternative forms. As a result, although she was from Holland, she came to County Clare to get a particular form of alternative therapy. However, on one of her trips to County Clare the GP sent her into the hospice. On her left breast, she had the worst fungating tumour that I had ever seen. At that stage, although she was only forty years of age, examination showed that the cancer had spread to her liver.

I met Kristen for the first time in a small two-bedded section of a busy surgical ward in Limerick. I had heard repeatedly over the weekend about the nursing and medical concern at her level of pain and social circumstances.

On meeting her I was struck by how curled up she was sitting on the bed, and by the pallor of her face and the beauty of her smile. She had a fifteen-month-old baby as well as nine- and six-year-old girls. The two older girls were in Holland, the baby was in the pram being pushed by her husband Reese. Kristen agreed to be transferred to the Palliative Care Unit and said she had become more spiritual since she got cancer and she was grateful for her cancer. She was also very realistic, but was still hoping for a cure. She said she was being true to herself in not having chemotherapy. She realised that she might die of cancer because of her choice, but there was a higher purpose. Her plans now were to move to Ireland and to bring her children and settle them in Ireland.

During her stay in the Palliative Care Unit she was in great form, but her pain was severe. At one stage in April she undressed with our help to reveal – unembarrassed – a necrotic, fungating left breast. There was no breast left, it was just a mass of gangrenous, flopping skin. She said during that conversation, 'I've been living in the wrong place, but the cancer has allowed me to do what I want to do and to go where I am meant to be.'

I remember her bent pale body, restless with pain, but with great eye contact and beautifully pale face and also the overwhelming smell. Her fifteen-month-old daughter was in the pushchair in the room being watched over by the staff of the unit. She said, 'I want to teach my children to follow their hearts, where they know inside where they need to be.' At the time in May I wrote:

> Healing is about balance not about cure.
> The lady nods with curved back and beauteous face.
> Blue-eyed blonde, her daughter Amadaya toddles and
> plots extravagances in the bathroom,
> emerging with a toilet cleaning brush.
> Tall flowers convert this sickroom into a Dutch cottage.
> Malignant pendulous mass leaks on her breast.
> Open mind dazed with opium.
> It is time to pray in this sacred place of lively rest.

Following that her pain became increased. She was short of breath, she became drowsy, she developed sickness, she began hallucinating and we dealt with each of these issues as best we could. Despite them all she was able to go out shopping with her children. Two days before she died I spoke to Kristen in the evening. She was crying about her mother, the fact that her mother was buying clothes for her children which she thought would be of poor quality and she wouldn't want to buy that type of clothes, but now her mother was taking over. About her own particular way of wanting to rear her children, about her direct, truthful personality, about wanting to discuss issues with her husband on his own and not having the opportunity. She spoke about the rhythm of nature and being in touch with this; about moments of great insight and joy the day before, and how the essence of life and death is very simple.

Why do I tell you these stories? It's not because I want to be morbid. What impact does caring for these people have on the team and the young doctors in training? How do we approach this time of staggering change where we stand balancing on the edge? It was a tradition among the Irish people in certain communities that if you were walking and saw a funeral procession moving along you joined in for a few steps and you said a certain prayer and you moved out. And that's what we do in palliative care, we join the procession for a few steps and then we move out. But to be able to be with change of such intensity requires not that you would walk in someone's shoes, but that you would take your own shoes off and walk barefoot.

TAKING RESPONSIBILITY IN A CHANGING WORLD

Ged Pierse

I am an engineer by background; chairman of a construction company by vocation. I am surrounded at home by people I love; at work by people I could not admire more, and upon whom I rely and trust completely to run a complex and multi-faceted business in a fast-moving and demanding world.

Life has been very good to me. I grew up in a warm, secure and loving Dalkey household; the second youngest of seven. Our roots were in North Kerry and we spent idyllic summers there in the forties and fifties.

The Christian Brothers in Monkstown sharpened my wits and awareness in the sleepy Ireland of the 1950s. Those post-war years were tough times in Ireland. Massive post-war reconstruction programmes in Britain offered employment and hope for many Irish men and women. The fifties and sixties were dismal decades of relentless emigration and general economic stagnation. The period was cemented together with a mix of hard-skinned determination, blind faith, old-style religion and other slow-moving certainties. I studied Engineering at UCD in the early 1960s and within weeks of graduation I took the boat to Holyhead with a beautiful new wife on my starboard side.

The first of our four daughters was born in 1966 and another Irish emigrant household took root on John Bull's mainland. We were in England for fourteen years. We missed Ireland. We missed the years away from our parents and the other family relationships; I missed the company of my Irish peers. But life moved on.

Those of us who are sufficiently ripe to remember post-war Ireland have moving pictures in our heads of the sodalities, the Corpus Christi processions whose marshals wore pioneer total abstinence pins. We can recall the reverence that was shown to authority in all its forms. Hats were removed when the priest passed on the street, in case he might have been carrying the Eucharist to a sick-bed. The sign of the cross was piously exercised passing the church or when a funeral procession moved by.

I came back to Ireland in 1977. Things were frugal still, but improving. I am an optimist. I bought a construction and engineering company called Public Works Ltd and later the Irish division of McInerney. Ireland was becoming embedded in the European Union. The influences and new disciplines were beginning to make their mark. The cattle were no longer traded on fair-day in the main street. Out at the marts the farmers were parking mud-splashed Land Rovers and powerful diesels.

The 1980s was a decade of steady, if uncertain, advance. If any times can be said to be innocent, they seem now in retrospect to have been innocent times by the standards of what was to follow.

After a sluggish start, the 1990s washed over us with a tidal wave of change. We were like sitting ducks. America started to lift the pace on the globalisation of their lifestyle. Michael Jackson, Bill Gates, Bill Clinton, Pamela Anderson, Madonna, Britney Spears. We were like blotting paper; we soaked it up. Relatively speaking, here in Ireland, we gave as good as we got; punched above our weight, as they say. We exported U2, Sinead

O'Connor, Riverdance, Elan, CRH, Bank of Ireland, AIB, Kerry Group, Baltimore Technologies, Anglo Irish Bank, the International Financial Services Centre. We won the Eurovision Song Contest.

We were hypnotised by the bright lights, drowned in a sea of cash and credit, electrified by the false promises of prosperity. The news made depressing reading; it seemed like crime, drunkenness and drug abuse were on the increase.

It smothered us before we could react. The Gardaí wrestled with the godfathers as best they could. They culled the leadership a few times. No sooner were these murderous thugs imprisoned or exiled than their shoes were filled by even more ruthless and heartless gangsters. They murdered Veronica Guerin. Today they launder their money through lap-dancing clubs.

The sounds of screaming and breaking glass, the howls of brawlers are the music now of the main street of every city, town and suburb in Ireland on Friday and Saturday nights. The side streets are no-go areas.

An *Irish Times*/TNS-MRBI poll published in September 2003 revealed that in Ireland, three out of five fifteen- to seventeen-year-olds drink alcohol and that, on what is defined in the research as 'a good night out', these minors consume on average eight drinks. The research also found that 44 per cent of fifteen- to twenty-four-year-olds have tried illegal drugs. At times it seems that Ireland is drowning in a sea of alcohol.

Over four hundred years ago the poet, John Milton wrote:

> The hungry sheep look up and are not fed
> but swol'n with rank mist they draw
> rot inwardly.

Was Milton foreseeing the Ireland of today?

But the truth is that we took our eye off the ball. The truth is we did not keep the children in check. The truth is we let our children drown in our national drink culture. The truth is we went into denial.

Fyodor Dostoevsky, writing in the nineteenth century, modelled his character Prince Myshkin in *The Idiot* on Jesus Christ. He proposed that truth was the most powerful thing in the world. The Prince always told the truth. It all ends in idiocy, darkness and tragedy, but it is not the Idiot who is wrong, it is a rotten Russia. It is a long time since I read Dostoevsky. I read the dust jacket to refresh my memory ...

> *The Idiot*, written in 1868 under appalling personal circumstances when Dostoevsky was travelling around Europe, not only reveals the author's acute artistic sense and psychological insight, but also affords his most penetrating indictment of a Russia struggling to emulate contemporary Europe and sinking under the weight of Western Materialism.

Sounds familiar.

Armed with my life experience and faced with our proposition here today, I believe that if we are to put things right in Irish society, and as an optimist I believe we can, then we must get back to the truth. We must harness the truth to give effect to change. We must take our heads out of the sand.

A little-known Irish writer called Francis Hackett resigned a prestigious and well-paid job as editor of a leading New York literary magazine and returned to Ireland in 1921 with his wife. They came to Ireland deliberately to contribute to the Irish literary revival. They wrote a number of books; she wrote on spiritualism and gynaecology; his were lighter commentaries on social issues. They were all banned. They left Ireland for good in the mid-twenties. Francis Hackett once wrote that the Irish were allergic to truth, facts and criticism. I believe that if we are to make progress in the world, we might do well to revisit Francis Hackett's observation and try to deal with it.

Our problems are not entirely home-grown. The truth is that there has been a steep decline in standards across the western world. America has been rocked by corporate scandals. Some of the major companies in the world were guilty of false accounting, resulting in their shareholders and workers being swindled out of billions of dollars. It is said that in the last five years middle-class America has lost over 7 trillion dollars due to corporate malpractice. WorldCom, Tyco and Enron are dramatic examples, but they are symptomatic of the professional tolerance of suspect values that threatened to collapse the investment world. These were the 'barbarians at the gate'. As a result people lost faith in companies, their auditors and the regulatory authorities.

Enron was run by a Chief Executive called Kenneth Lay. He was and is still one of President Bush's closest advisors and was a major financial contributor to Bush's Presidential Campaign. Enron, a conglomerate, was regarded as one of the blue-chip companies of America. One of its principal areas of trading was in the electricity business and it ran most of the power grids of Eastern America. For years Enron lost money but reported bumper profits with the collusion of their auditors, Arthur Andersen. In the eighties and nineties, Arthur Andersen was one of the most respected auditing companies in the world, with a reputation for excellence, honesty and truthfulness. Investors and regulatory authorities thought they could rely on their imprimatur. Despite Bush's attempts to prop up Enron for Lay, Enron collapsed overnight and 65 billion was lost by shareholders. In the fallout that ensued it was discovered that Arthur Andersen had been party to falsifying the annual reports of the company and Andersen was sued worldwide. They did not have the resources to meet all the claims and they too had to fold.

The regulatory authorities in America moved quickly to ensure that auditing and accounting standards were properly enforced in corporate America. They put severe penalties on the shoulders of Chief Executives and Directors who did not accept their responsibilities to see that the accounts of their companies were fairly presented. Almost overnight a large proportion of corporate America withdrew their previous year's accounts and later returned to the markets with restated and reduced profits. It was as if the system was purging itself of its guilt and that is just as well, because had it not, the whole basis of capitalism in America would have been threatened. Trust had to be restored, because without trust, the business and financial world cannot perform or relate. It was a wake-up call for the professionals in America to sort out their business ethics and to pull back from the rampant materialism and greed structures that had driven the American system in the previous twenty years.

The Enron/Arthur Andersen debacle reverberated around all the global financial markets and as a result the regulatory authorities in most civilised countries have introduced additional responsibilities and penalties in relation to corporate governance. In Ireland a new Bill, 'The Companies Auditing & Accounting Bill 2003' was published in February last. This requires all public companies, whether listed or not, to establish an audit committee. The bill requires that an audit committee should have at least two members, none of whom is an employee or chairman of the company, and lays down rigid criteria to ensure the independence of an audit committee member. Similar legislation has been introduced in the UK and it's felt that it is only a question of time before large private companies will also be required to have independent audit committees. Capitalism recognises that you cannot do business without trust.

The reality of change in the corporate world is that the fundamentals never change. The integrity of the entire system is based on trust. It is somewhat akin to the self-assessment income tax system in that the regulatory authorities can only test a tiny fraction of companies for compliance with the standard statements of accountancy practice. They rely heavily on the professional institutions and their disciplinary bodies to see that corporate law is upheld. The two professions that bear the greatest responsibility in this respect are the accountancy/audit and the legal professions. When these professions are more concerned with the quality of their fees rather than the quality of their governance, the whole fabric of the system is threatened. Hopefully the Enron/Arthur Andersen debacle has put the system on notice and the professions have learnt the lesson.

Richard A. Grasso, CEO of the New York Stock Exchange recently wrote:

> The integrity and openness of the market must be trustworthy. We are doing our very best to make sure that it stays that way. Trust is the keystone of our business.

In recent years we have had a number of tribunals and enquiries to investigate such matters as planning, the beef industry, the abuse of children, infected blood. We are all aware of the detail and somewhat bored or numbed by it all now. The real casualties of these tribunals have been truth and trust. Day after day, week after week, month after month, people perjure themselves with the aid of their legal advisors to such an extent that one must query the compliance of some of our professional practitioners and their regulatory bodies.

I believe the public has lost confidence in the legal profession in Ireland. To a great extent it has lost faith in the legal system in Ireland.

I believe the public doesn't trust our accountancy bodies, our banks and our financial institutions and they have every good reason not to. Hopefully the changes in the 2003 Finance Act will help to address this, but the public view the wide scale tax evasion, the malpractice by the banks and overcharging by the legal profession with some disdain.

Our politicians have lost the trust of the voters. When I was a young man the turnout in a General Election would be over 75 per cent. Today in critical European elections the poll can be as low as 30 per cent of the electorate. This again is symptomatic of the lack of trust and apathy towards authority. If we are honest with ourselves we must realise that the Ireland of today is in serious trouble. The Portuguese have a saying 'a fish rots from its head down'; I believe that we have suffered from weak Government in this country for a number of years. I don't blame the individuals, I blame the system. The concentration has been on political survival rather than on proper government; on the cult and myth of personality instead of proper policies and actions.

We have a legal and accountancy system that spends the majority of its time trying to circumvent the laws rather than administer them properly. We have had a disgraceful teachers' strike, a guards' strike and a hospital strike, which should not be tolerated in a civilised society. We fail to teach civics and respect for our environment in our schools, which results in our landscape being vandalised by litter and graffiti. We have filthy towns and cities. We refuse to face our responsibilities in relation to waste disposal. We have a collapsing health service and the most expensive housing in Europe.

No wonder as a nation we drink too much.

Have we learnt from our mistakes? Are we changing our ways? Are we taking responsibility? The optimist in me says 'Yes'. In the last twelve months the tide has started to turn, ably assisted I must say by institutes like Céifin. Things will be corrected in due course. Our political leaders are beginning to realise that you cannot run a country by perceptions. There are signs of reforms in public administration and hopefully a lasting peace in the North is within our grasp.

There can be a tendency to overstate the negative on occasions like this at the expense of balance. Good news does not sell. But I am a firm believer in the great balance in nature;

the oak's parabola. The ozone layer is repairing. The water quality in Dublin Bay is set to dramatically improve following the completion of a waste-treatment system for which our firm was the main contractor. I have great faith in human nature and in my fellow countrymen and women. I believe that despite serious slippage in standards, despite the gravity of self-interest, we will snap out of this unhappy malaise.

The stock markets are slowly recovering giving some evidence that trust is being rebuilt. A new honesty is emerging in the press in relation to the nation's alcoholism. At last we seem to have the capacity to recognise that these problems exist. The next decade will judge how we measure up to the new reality and repair the damage of the last ten years.

If the audience here present in Ennis today is evidence of the responsible fabric of contemporary Irish society, and I believe it is, then my optimism has grounds.

Again John Milton comes to mind –

And now by some strong motion I am led
Into this wilderness; to what intent
I learn not yet. Perhaps I need not know;
For what concerns my knowledge God reveals.

SYSTEMS AND POWER:
EXPLORING THE ECOLOGY OF CHANGE

Paula Downey

Some years ago, when I began to discover what was happening to our planet, I felt distinctly troubled. It wasn't sudden or dramatic, more a creeping unease, a growing sense that all is not well with the world.

Melting ice caps and rising sea levels. Changing weather patterns, soil erosion, loss of species. Disappearing rain forests. Famine. Drought. Terrible poverty. Wars. Slavery. Problems with food, spreading disease, rocketing population and much more. The more I learnt, the more I questioned, and the more my unease turned to sheer frustration. It's called the burden of awareness, I think. Knowing, but also sensing that it's all too big and unmanageable – we've all been there.

I felt there were infinitely more questions than answers. And I felt no one in particular was that pushed about answering the questions. I began to doubt what I was being told. By the media. By politicians. By business. And I started to become aware of a yawning gap between what was presented as the truth, and what I understood from my own investigation and study to be the reality, and my frustration turned into anger.

When you begin to see things differently there's no going back. And what I noticed most of all was how the mainstream media that washes over us all in so many ways every day, never seems to join the dots between for example: climate change and the pursuit of economic growth, or the poverty of some nations and the wealth of others and many other missed connections.

How easily we miss the fact that everything is linked. The power of the corporate voice in shaping government policy, the lowering of taxation and the decline in public services, are all linked. The chronic rise in pollution of every kind, the premeditated waste of our consumer culture, the decimation of finite natural resources, and the rise of global brands – these are all linked. Our sense of disconnection from each other and from nature, the rise in crime and social disorder, and the alarming fall-off in public participation in the democratic process. These are all connected.

What can seem like separate phenomena are in fact patterns, the same predictable punch line repeated over and over again in a multitude of ways throughout our lives. But the connections aren't made. Business drags its feet on making any meaningful response. Politicians side-step the issues. The media maintains a safe distance. And collectively *we don't act*. We behave as if nothing is wrong! Public discourse churns on and on playing the same old tunes. You'd certainly never guess we are on the brink of a global crisis many scientists and others in the know tell us is shaping up to threaten our very survival as a species. And not at some distant point thousands of years down the road, either. Soon. This century. Possibly, even in the lifetime of many of us in this room.

Who is to blame for this nightmare? I wanted to know. Who is responsible for this monumental mess we've got ourselves into? I wanted to find the culprits, and confront them. *I wanted blood!*

All of this had been germinating in my mind and when the time came to research my thesis for a Master's in Responsibility and Business Practice at Bath University, I decided my chance had arrived. I would use the opportunity to go find the culprits and tackle them about what I saw as an obvious collusion between business, politics, and the media. I decided my task should be to meet with leaders in all of these institutions, and I set to work.

I went to what I thought were the seats of power: chief executives in business, political representatives, newspaper editors, high profile journalists and senior broadcast executives, and my question was simple: 'Knowing what we know, why don't *you* act?'

What I discovered was startling. Much to my disappointment, these high-flying, super-charged, management types were ordinary people just like me! And what's more, I discovered many of them were quite ignorant of the issues, and those who weren't felt just as trapped, just as fearful – and every bit as incapable of putting things right – as everyone else. So no, I didn't discover any culprits out there. I didn't discover that someone was to blame. Or even some people. I discovered something else. Something bigger and immensely more important.

I discovered that we live and work in a system of power that is real, the net effect of which is to keep us economically productive and politically docile and limited in our sense of what it is we are here to do – other than go shopping. I also discovered that this system operates with our collusion – indeed it is kept in place *only* by our willingness to buy its message. To believe.

That's why I believe we will engage more effectively in bringing about change if we take a systems view of how things happen. Learning to understand how the world works at a more subtle level, how the dynamics of the system impinge on all of us, and in particular how power protects the status-quo, will help us to be more discerning about how we choose to act in any given situation and how we engage in changing the things we want to change. And that's what I'd like to talk about this morning. I want to explore the ecology of change.

Why do we buy the message so completely? Why *do* we support a system that's doing so much damage? Maybe it's because we don't see it. It's invisible. We just don't see that we're part of a system.

The anthropologist Gregory Bateson said:

> All the major problems in the world are the result of the difference between the way nature works and the way man thinks.

He was suggesting that our real problem is a problem of perception. The difference between 'reality' and how we see the world. And more particularly how we humans see our place in it. So maybe what we have is not so much an ecological problem, or even an economic problem, but a problem – *a crisis* – of the mind?

How *do* we see the world?

I think we see it 'out there' somewhere. Separate from us. We're here, and everything else is 'out there'. And every*one* else is 'out there'. We simply don't see our connectedness to every*one* and every*thing* else.

To understand where this sense of separateness comes from we have to take a short trip back in time, to our transition from a nomadic lifestyle when we went wherever the food was, to a settled life in which we exerted control over our food supply. Whereas mankind's story had been one of connectedness – a sense of *participation with* nature's rhythms, the new story was about *control over* nature. And that story grew to see Man as the pinnacle of evolution and everything else – plants, birds, animals, insects and all of nature's wealth – as resources for Man's exclusive use.

This 'separateness' mindset that developed alongside the idea of agriculture, was later compounded by the emergence of early science with its mechanistic world view. Science was successful. Its view prevailed, and ultimately came to dominate our entire western culture, as it does to this day. We think we are so progressive and sophisticated and modern, yet the way we think about things is still largely based on a set of assumptions identified by people like Isaac Newton and his contemporaries more than *three hundred and fifty years ago!* Our way of seeing is really quite old-fashioned.

When Isaac Newton looked at the night sky, he saw a vast, infinite space that he believed was empty except for the stars and planets. And on this belief he built an understanding of a world in which the *physical* elements, the things we can touch and see – mountains, rivers and seas, our bodies, our buildings – were the basic buildings blocks of existence.

When the famous apple fell from the tree he conceived of 'gravity' as a force that emanated from one source and acted on another, like billiard balls: the white strikes the blue, causing the blue to strike the yellow and so on. And it was the combination of this 'cause-and-effect' thinking, together with a focus on the physical world, that brought Newton to conceive of the universe as a clockwork machine. A 'tick-tock, tick-tock' universe in which the physical parts interact in a mechanical, linear, chain-of-events-cause-and-effect way. This happens, so that happens. And even though science has long since updated this world view, we still allow it to completely dominate our lives in so many ways.

Two hundred years after Newton, Albert Einstein found that the poster child of this mechanical way of thinking was only partly right, for Einstein saw the physical elements too, but he also saw what was in between them. Einstein discovered that space is not empty at all, but filled with fields of energy that structure the space in which things happen.

Einstein's genius was to point to *the power of the invisible.* He suggested the basic building blocks of the universe are not the physical stuff at all, but these invisible fields of energy, and the stuff we normally focus all our attention on – the things we *can* see – are really secondary effects of these fields of energy. What really matters, Einstein felt, is the *relationship* between the physical elements because what happens in that space is what makes the physical elements what they are. For example, what happens in the relationship between me and say my brother or my mother, is what makes me what I am, and makes them what they are, in the context of that relationship.

Einstein then went one step further, and suggested that there aren't any building blocks at all! Things don't exist as independent things or components, but only *in relation* to something else. If we transfer this concept into our everyday world we can see, for example, that doctors only exist in relation to patients. Patients only exist in relation to doctors. No patients, no doctor. No doctor, no patients. No students, no teacher. No teacher, no students. Here today, I am only called forth as a speaker, because you are good enough to listen. And you are only called forth as listeners because I am speaking. No listener, no speaker. No speaker, no listener.

So, science tells us the world isn't 'out there' somewhere. We call it forth. We call forth the whole world as we enter into relationship with it and with each other. And if we swap Isaac Newton's lens for Albert Einstein's, we can see that our world is *not* a machine, but a complex *web* of relationship in which infinite numbers of relationships overlap and combine to determine the kind of world we experience. What we're talking about here, of course, is a system.

This conference is concerned with the reality of change, and how we can do things differently. I would like to suggest that the first thing we have to do is change our ideas about change itself. To stop seeing the world as a clockwork machine, and start seeing it as a non-linear, complex web of overlapping relationships. As a system. And it's alive. It's a *living* system. Constantly in the process of creation.

I'd like to mention just a few of the basic principles of complex living systems which I think we need to be aware of as we try to make change happen.

Perhaps the most important thing to understand is that complex systems aren't 'made'. Living systems are self-making. No one's in charge and there's no hierarchy. No boss. Complex systems make themselves. The system brings itself to life as the components of the system help to make each other: I help to make my brother what he is. He helps to make me what I am. Our relationship helps to make our family what it is. And the family helps to make each one of us. And because we live in nested systems – systems within systems within systems – our family helps to make the system that is our neighbourhood and our neighbourhood helps to make the system that is our city and so on.

Systems make themselves by taking information from the environment and responding to it. Information is the key ingredient in life because information organises life, or rather, it helps life to self-organise. And *new* information helps living systems to evolve. Hopefully, when this conference is over you'll have some new information, and that information will help you evolve in some way. Without new information nothing new can happen, so new information is essential to changing the system. And in human systems information includes actions, behaviours and choices as well as data.

Secondly, despite the fact that no-one's in charge and systems make themselves, they don't necessarily descend into anarchy and chaos, do they? The world today is very much like the world that showed up yesterday. Go to work, and the workplace you experience today is pretty much the same workplace you experienced yesterday. Look at a photograph of yourself as a two-year-old, and look in the mirror today. The 'you' you were then looks very much like the 'you' you are now. A little worn, a little torn, but still much the same.

Why is that? How is it that if – as we know it to be the case – our skin is renewed every month and our liver every six weeks, how is it we don't morph into a dog, or a tree, or some other person? The answer is simple. At the heart of every system, there's an identity – a story or sense of what it is supposed to become. And in the process of coming to life a living system constantly refers to its story, filtering new information through it as it recreates itself. And it's just the same whether we're talking about our bodies, our organisations and institutions, or the wider society. There is a story at the heart of the system.

And then there are the terrible twins of order and chaos. While most of us would probably feel that life as we experience it up-close is a bit chaotic, it's actually far from chaotic. It is in fact, full of order and full of patterns. In systems language these patterns are called 'fractals'. Shapes that repeat themselves right throughout the system, at many different levels. Take a tree for example. Look at its overall shape and then look at the shape of its parts – the branching and leaf clusters – and you'll notice that even the smallest twigs display the same pattern as the whole tree. This is an example of fractals at work.

Information taken into the system forms a pattern over time and repeats itself at every level. This is a metaphor for all of life, when you consider how small amounts of information repeated over time can shift a whole community in the direction of a new value. And it happens without our noticing, and without anyone in charge. No conductor of the orchestra. The system makes and remakes itself. And it's the same everywhere, in our families, in our workplaces. In my consulting work with organisations, I can tell you that when I walk into almost any company I will find the same pattern of behaviour I experience at the front desk, repeated throughout the company at every level. Even walking from office to office you can sense these patterns.

And finally, there's feedback. If we want to change things it's very important to understand feedback. The system responds to information via the infinite number of overlapping and interconnected feedback channels in the web of relationship.

Positive feedback amplifies new information and changes the system and sometimes even a tiny change can snowball and bring about big differences. Negative feedback, on the other hand, dampens down new information and keeps the system within certain boundaries, which explains why so often, in spite of new information in the system, nothing changes.

So when Gregory Bateson said all the major problems in the world stem from the difference between the way *nature* works and the way man *thinks*, I believe he meant that we *think* of the world as a machine rather than as a system. We believe it's predictable, manageable, measurable, knowable and linear, when the truth is we're living in a largely *un*predictable, *un*manageable, *un*measurable, *un*knowable, *non*-linear *system*.

It's this way of seeing the world that makes us break things up into smaller pieces in our efforts to control, manage and measure, and change things. Yet systems science tells us that if we want to understand a complex system we need to look at the whole thing – the bigger picture – the patterns and the relationships.

There's another very important dimension of social systems we must pay attention to if we're interested in changing things, and that's power. Power shapes our world. The moment there's more than one person, there are issues of power because power is the mechanism by which things get decided. That's simply how we do Life. Power is far from simple. It operates in many different ways and takes many different forms, and in my experience people find it helpful to be able to 'see' power, to be able to name it and point to it when they see it operating, because it explains a lot of what's going on in our world.

So in exploring this ecology of change I'd like to present you with a palette of some of the more prevalent kinds of power we experience. What follows isn't a hierarchy of power, rather I will try to work from the more obvious to the more subtle and very potent forms of power.[1]

Let's begin with what I will call Power 1.

Power 1 is the power of veto. This dimension is about who wins in decision-making. It's the power that says: I have power over you or you have power over me, to the extent that one of us can get the other to do something we mightn't otherwise do.

Examples of this power are everywhere throughout our lives. When an employer instructs an employee to work late or work the weekend and there's no discussion. Although he has other plans the employee co-operates because he doesn't want to be identified as difficult or uncooperative. That's Power 1.

When a teacher keeps a student back after school, Power 1 is at work. It's there when a parent tells a child: eat your dinner or you won't get any dessert. Or, do your homework or you won't go out to play. Each of these are moments of life we can recognise and each is an exercise in power of one person over another. Power 1 is about observable winners and losers and it's a view that captures the attention of much of our news media. We are told about who's fighting, and who's winning: the government minister versus the lobby group. The protestors versus the organisation. The company versus the Union. The environmentalist versus the developer ... and so on

When we believe that we can tell who's more or less powerful in a society by studying observable behaviour, we are assuming that power is all about conflict that's out in the open. But that's not always the case, and that brings us to the next dimension of Power – the power that prevents conflict emerging at all.

What I'm calling Power 2 operates when a person or a group consciously or unconsciously works to block conflict from coming into the open. The power that controls what's discussed, and what's not discussed. The power that organises some issues 'in' to public discourse, and organises other issues 'out'.

We see Power 2 at work when there's a meeting before the real meeting to decide what will be on the agenda and what will be 'off limits' at the real meeting. This is about mobilising bias in the system, dampening down information to keep potential issues from becoming actual issues. Power 2 is all about influence and authority. It's about coercion and manipulation of one kind or another, though it may not always be consciously motivated.

Governments and BigBusiness use Power 2 all the time. For example when a radio or television interviewee doesn't answer the question or, as frequently happens, answers a different question. By not picking up the ball they're blocking the issue from getting onto the table at all. This is not just about 'not answering the question' – it's an exercise in power.

News and editorial decision-making in the media is all about Power 2. The production of knowledge through research – a critical issue in shaping our world – is subject to Power 2 when it comes to deciding what gets funded and researched, and what doesn't. Most public relations work now commonly referred to as 'spin' is power at work.

In the run up to the Johannesburg Earth Summit, so much lobbying and influencing of the agenda by the business world was going on, that one of the senior organisers went public a month before the conference to warn people not to expect anything very useful to come of the deliberations. As he put it, the outcome had already been hijacked. That was all about Power 2.

But what if it's not that obvious? What I'm calling Power 1 and Power 2 focus on behaviour we can see. Observable conflict or the suppression of it. This supposes that people know where their interests lie and that there's an assumption that if they don't complain out loud or demonstrate any sense of injustice, their interests are not being harmed. But what if people aren't aware of their interests in the first place? How could they complain then? Wouldn't the supreme exercise of power be to shape perceptions and preferences so that no sense of injustice is even felt?

Is it possible that the public inertia we witness in relation to many of the hugely critical issues of our time, which we blithely put down to apathy, is perhaps a clue to a more subtle and deep-rooted power at work? David Edwards has said: 'The ultimately secure system of control is one that presents every appearance of complete freedom – for who then would perceive any need to challenge it?'[2]

This brings us to Power 3.

Just by our experience most of us can easily accept that people do exercise power over others, and people do control agendas everywhere, in business, politics, the community generally. People often have their own personal agendas. Power 3 suggests that this controlling of the agenda is not only in the hands of individuals, but embedded in the pattern of relationships and social arrangements that we live and work within. In other words, power has biased the way things are organised in the system in the first place.

Power 3 controls the entire system by controlling the ideas and relationships that shape the system itself. This is not only about you exercising power over me, getting me to do something I don't want to do. It's about influencing what I want and what I don't want. Advertising is clearly a component of this power, preaching the commercial gospel day and night, night and day: 'success' looks like this ... 'youth' looks like this ... 'old age' looks like this ... 'work' looks like this ... 'happiness' looks like this ... 'love' looks like this ... 'living' looks like this ... Repeating our story, over and over, and over again.

But of course it's not only about advertising. Power 3 works in many ways to shape public discourse, for example by ensuring that the concept of economic growth as an appropriate singular goal for a whole society is broadly supported and never publicly questioned. It's the power that shapes us by influencing the ways we are socialised, colouring our sense of who we are, what we should aspire to and what life is for. It's the power that shapes the *non*-production of information: what we don't know and what we don't discover, the reports that aren't commissioned, the investigations that don't take place, the issues that don't get on to the agenda and so on.

When you wonder why things *don't* happen, or why things *don't* change, Power 3 is almost certainly lurking in the background. It's hard to see because it is not a discrete act or a specific behaviour, or even a conscious strategy. It's a *system* of power that is the product of common interests and overlapping relationships between certain processes and components in our social system.

For example, media ownership. The trend – or *pattern* – of media ownership is towards consolidation so more and more newspapers, radio and tv channels are finding themselves in fewer and fewer hands. In other words the source of the story is narrowing. Owners of media conglomerates often point to a range of perspectives across their titles to claim non-bias, but one leading figure in Irish journalism said to me: 'What *is* uniform right across the board, is what's *not* covered.' Classic Power 3!

Just recently an entire supplement on climate change in the *Sunday Independent* included everything you ever wanted to know about changing weather patterns and the effect on insurance claims, but not a single word about what might be causing this pending global and human catastrophe. No link – no *hint* of a connection – between our fossil-fuelled global economic model with its gluttonous quest for continuous economic growth, and the gathering storm clouds of climate change.

The dots are never joined, because to do that would be to question the story itself. And ultimately, question ourselves.

As media outlets become business conglomerates, commercial pressures take hold: Grow market share! Cut costs! Increase profit! Satisfy shareholders! This pressure to maximise sales, viewership, circulation and advertising revenue guarantees that celebrity and trivia, and so-called popular entertainment, will be chosen to fill the pages or the airtime rather than any serious and sustained coverage of complex or tricky issues like climate change, world poverty, the globalisation of capital or even HIV/AIDS.

In addition, advertisers quite naturally support media whose editorial opinion is business friendly, and since newspapers are subsidised by advertising to the tune of approximately 75 per cent, it's a no-brainer that those that support the status-quo survive and thrive, while those whose editorial line is challenging to the status-quo must rely on funding from a much smaller pool: patrons, subscribers, supporters and volunteers. And often they don't survive.

And so the voice of the status-quo dominates and endures, while the space for alternative views remains narrow and in the margins. And so long as what appears to be an overwhelming consensus is maintained, it's easy to dismiss those with alternative points of view as oddballs, eco-warriors, pinko-lefties, eccentrics, the lunatic fringe or whatever you're having yourself. So despite the fact that we've never had so many sources of media in this so-called information age, we get a remarkably unified 'story'.

This is further compounded by pressure on resources in the media. In the race to cut costs and maximise shareholder returns, most media businesses can't afford the luxury of having staff out in the world discovering the news. As a result, much of the news originates from government spokespeople, or public relations press releases. The media is also evermore dependent on 'free' content or cheap content, or secondhand content, so we have the modern phenomenon of presenters sitting in radio studios talking to other presenters in other studios telling listeners what they can see on Sky News or CNN!

You can surf the dial today and find more or less the same news on every station. This wouldn't happen in a healthier, more diverse system, but because of commercial pressures, the information in our social system has become a process of promoting and defending the interests of the economically and politically powerful, while *simultaneously* 'dampening down' many other alternative voices and interests. It sounds like a conspiracy, but it's not a conspiracy. It's not even about overt control.

To try and explain how it works I'd like to borrow a chemistry experiment used to explain how snowflakes are made.[3] I want you to imagine a large square frame, like a biscuit-tin lid. Let's say it's six feet square and the sides are six inches high. Now imagine a chute sitting just above the square frame, and down the chute pour hundreds of tennis balls right into the square frame. What will happen? What will the end result of that process be?

The result is inevitable: they'll build an almost perfect pyramid shape because there's no other way for round tennis balls to settle on this structure other than in the shape of a pyramid. The most stable position for any tennis ball is one that builds the structure and most of them will settle in this way, while the others will simply bounce off and be lost.

Similarly, if we swap the square frame for a circular frame and pour the tennis balls into that frame the result will not be a pyramid, but a mound, because that's the only shape possible if you pour round tennis balls into a round frame. The point is, the tennis balls respond to the frame. The structure they build depends on the shape of the frame. No one is controlling it. The shape is simply the inevitable result of the framing conditions.

This analogy illustrates that the real power in society lies with those who determine the basic framing ideas of our society: our purpose, our goals, our values and what we strive for. Together, the government of the day and powerful elites create the framing ideas: *maximise economic growth via a system of private corporations, fuelled by a system of mass production, fuelled by mass consumption* ... then, like the tennis balls in our experiment, the news and information, people, organisations, ideas, choices and decisions that support the framing ideas wriggle themselves into stable positions on the pyramid, while the more challenging or dissenting ones fall off and are lost.

In other words as our collective communicative behaviour is 'poured' over the framework of governing ideas, the behaviour that conforms to the pattern or structure of the pyramid, sticks, while the rest disappear off into the margins. That's Power 3. It's not a conspiracy. What we get is simply the inevitable result of the fundamental framing ideas. The ideas that we allow to become our 'common sense'. Our Story.

It all seems a bit depressing, doesn't it? The system seems so sewn up, so comprehensively sewn up. No escape hatch. No way out. But in spite of the enormous power that keeps things the same, things do change. So if you and I want to make change happen, as well as understanding the dynamic that keeps things the same, we need to understand how change happens.

Power 1, 2 and 3 as I've described them, all have one thing in common: each of them sees power as Power Over. In other words, power as *descendent* ... percolating down from one 'sovereign' or another, 'up there' somewhere. The Boss. The Government. The CEO. The Shareholder. The Expert. This way of thinking about power is a hangover from the sovereign-subject relationships of feudal times and while we have been gradually replacing monarchies and dictatorships with 'democratic' parliaments, we haven't changed our mind-set. We haven't finished the democracy project anywhere, so when we want to see power we still 'look up'. The idea of the world as a hierarchy is still dominant in our view of the world.

In some ways, we cherish our sense of limitation believing that only 'they' have power, or that 'power is bad'. But this view of reality that places power outside ourselves and beyond our reach is inherently self-defeating, and self-fulfilling. Because the power*less* create a vacuum that the power*ful* step into and fill.

If we stop seeing the world as a hierarchy or a machine and begin to see it instead as a system, we can see the circular relationship between the components and the system – how the components make each other, and make the system itself.

From a systems perspective, we can't stop at Power Over. We must dig deeper to find another layer to our understanding of power. And to do that, we have to finally let go of the legacy of Newtonian science, the old paradigm view of the 'world-as-machine', because this prevents us from engaging fully with the dynamics of the universe.

In Newton's view of things, to make change you have to fight might with might. You need weight and acceleration to create sufficient mass, to topple the status-quo. But Einstein and modern physicists teach us that the world is far more sensitive than that. It's a system. A web of connection and relationship, and it's alive. So we're not working with a clockwork machine. In fact, we're not working with matter at all. We're working with *energy*, and energy doesn't behave like matter.

Information, ideas and meaning are energies. They can travel at great speed and appear as potent forces that have totally surprising and often unexpected results. If we remember that changes in the physical world are just the secondary effects of changes in processes that are invisible, we start to recognise the critical role of information rippling through life's feedback loops. Size of effort is not the issue when it comes to change in a system.

What I have labelled Power 3 illustrates that ideas are not just powerful, but *astonishingly* powerful fields of energy that easily control our patterns of behaviour. In a self-organising universe information is the key resource that brings matter into form. Without it, nothing happens, and without new information nothing new is possible.

Because of the way feedback works in complex and non-linear systems, even slight variances can amplify in unanticipated ways. New information – or *difference* – disturbs the peace and if the difference is identified as meaningful, it's a potent force for change. In a systems world, anything that creates a disturbance plays a crucial role in goading a system to self-organise into a new form, so making 'difference' is critical.

Small acts of difference can have powerful effects, such as when we express our convictions courageously even if they seem daft in terms of the prevailing 'common sense'. Or when we dare to make a challenging comment at a meeting when the norm would be to stay silent. (I don't mean being disruptive, but being constructively challenging by for example asking a different kind of question.) Or when we make a new choice in our personal lifestyle that others can witness, or we choose not to support the majority view.

In a systems world, these acts of difference have the potential to grow. The system will choose to accept or reject the new information and respond, and if it's meaningful to the system it will bring the new information inside itself where it will adapt and adjust and mutate as it moves through the feedback loops and amplifies the disturbance in unpredictable ways. When they create a disturbance the system can no longer ignore, real change is possible and the conditions that enable it to flip to a whole new place magically appear. This was the case with the Berlin Wall where, what appeared to be a sudden act, was in fact the outcome of very many small acts occurring within an unbroken wholeness, over decades. Each small act of defiance, or new way of thinking or behaving, invisibly connected to other small acts ... growing, mutating, changing, *amplifying* ... until suddenly the system 'jumped' to a completely new place.

Robert Kennedy described this phenomenon when he said:

> Each time a person stands up for an idea, or acts to improve the lot of others, or strikes out against injustice, (s)he sends forth a tiny ripple of hope, and crossing each other from a million different centres of energy and daring, those ripples build a current that can sweep down the mightiest walls of oppression and resistance.

As we work to bring about change in a living system, we're working with webs of relationship. What matters are the *kinds* of connections in the web, and the availability of places to exchange energy and ideas, like this conference right here, today. In a web, we influence the entire system by working right where we are, with the system we know. From a Newtonian perspective our efforts might seem small and we may doubt our actions make any difference. Or if our view is Darwinian, we might hope our small efforts will somehow contribute incrementally to a large-scale evolution.

The quantum view explains the success of small efforts quite differently. It suggests that no single component is the cause. In a networked, relational world all action is both local and global, and the potential impact of local actions is not related to their size or weight.

Local changes affect the global system not through incrementalism, but because every small system – like you and me – participates in an unbroken wholeness. Activities in one part of the system create effects that appear in distant places and we never know how our small activities affect others through the invisible fabric of our connectedness. In this connected world, it's never a question of 'critical mass'. It's always about *critical connections*. And potential for influence is everywhere, literally whenever and wherever two energies meet.

We've talked about Power 1, 2 and 3 as having Power Over, now I'd like to introduce two more kinds of power, which are quite different.

Power 4 is Power *With*. This is the power that springs up whenever people get together and act together. Social movements and activists are critical catalysts in helping to make the wider society aware of issues, but they're not the real force for change. Change happens when the wider general public reacts strongly to counteract powerful elites.

Power With means that power is a property of the system itself. It belongs to the group or system and it remains in existence as long as the group stays together. When we say that someone is 'in power' we mean she is temporarily empowered by a certain group of people to act in their name. However, the moment that group disappears her power also vanishes. The celebrated author and psychiatrist Scott Peck calls this 'Temporal Power' – power vested in the job or position, not in the person.

The organisations and institutions of this or any other nation remain in place only with our support and our consent. Like cupped hands holding sand, *we* hold them in place creating the illusion of power by the nature and quality of our attention, and in this we are greatly helped by the ongoing diligence of journalists and the mainstream media who, through their persistent focus on a narrow range of voices, constantly breathe life into what's called 'the establishment'. What we don't perhaps understand too readily, is that we can uncup our hands and withdraw our support at any time. That's our prerogative.

While Power Over is about descendent power – coming from the top – Power With is *ascendent* power that percolates up from people right throughout the system, and that's what ultimately transforms the system.

Power With is the power of the network. And we shouldn't be surprised that just at the moment when the dynamic of Power Over seems to have sewn up our world and it seems impossible to escape its grip, the network is emerging as a powerful counter-veiling force in all sorts of places, both face-to-face and in its technological expression across the internet. In a network, every member matters. Each one of us is at the centre. Responsibility passes through the web, leadership is shared. And crucially, we never know where we are in the network. You or I may be the critical link between different networks of knowledge or activity. Or we may be the last snowflake on the branch ... before it breaks.

Power With is the mechanism by which people who don't have economic or political power can bring influence to bear on the decisions of business and political leaders – after all, it's resistance that keeps Power 3 on its toes!

The worldwide anti-war marches and globalisation protests which seemed to spring from nowhere with no obvious leadership, are changing the agenda. Power percolating *up*. The international growth of consumer activist groups targeting the likes of MacDonald's, NIKE, Exxon, Monsanto and others, and drawing attention to the tobacco, oil, pharmaceutical, biotech and other industries are all examples of Power With. The citizens action against bin collection charges and literally hundreds of similar instances where people are taking responsibility and acting together are all examples of Power With.

The key message here is that in order to cause difference, we have to *do* something. Something *different*. We have to take action, participate, engage. And this brings me finally, to one last but hugely critical dimension of power: Power 5. The Power *Within*.

Power Within is the fuel in the engine of Power With. If power is more a process than a thing, and if power is everywhere in the system, then no one is powerless. Power is present in every moment of every day, and in every relationship. It shapes the micro-politics of every situation and that's why the nature of relationship is critical, and why the quality of our intention in that relationship, as well as the quality of our being, are so important. Each of us has power, so we also have responsibility – not just for the here-and-now, visible effects of our action or inaction, but for all the possible repercussions further down the line.

For there is no small act. Fractals teach us that in a systems world, the small things make the big things. The actions of real people form the repeated patterns that shape the world. Power Within is a quality that grows every time we choose to connect our deepest feelings and values – our inner world – to our actions *in* the world. Power Within is the power of living with integrity and every time we act with integrity we take control of the power in our lives.

Power Over, the power dynamic we are inside, keeps things the same ... but only as long as we don't see its hold on us. Power With and Power Within have the potential to change the world.

So what do we do, if we want to be part of this change? What are we prepared to do? The answer to that question is deeply personal, and you are going to answer it for yourselves. I'd like to offer some of my own thoughts, to help set that scene.

I think we need to liberate ourselves by seeing the story that traps us, and liberate others by helping them to do the same. We need to turn off the television, stop reading the same old newspapers and look for alternative sources of information to help develop a truer picture of the system we live in. We need to begin experiencing ourselves as part of a system, to see that the world is not 'out there, somewhere', but that we call it forth every moment of every day as we participate with it and with each other.

If you have radical doubts about our current story, make yourself visible, so that we can be visible to one another. It's time to stop feeling like the lunatic fringe and recognise that we're part of the fastest growing social group in western society. Indeed, the American sociologist Paul Ray, who's been doing research into culture and lifestyle for twenty years or more, tells us that some 50 million Americans and up to 120 million Europeans (including many in this room I suspect) don't feel their values and aspirations are represented in the current socio-economic story, so they're actively pursuing new ways of working and living and organising themselves. They're writing a new story. They are not seen by the current information system because that's organised to serve the status-quo. But they're there and for anyone interested in revitalising business or politics, they're the fastest growing and almost untapped market in the western world.

We need to get our act together. *Together*. We can't do what has to be done, alone. No generation ever before has faced the task we face now: to *consciously* evolve to a better place. Sure, we've evolved before, but we took time – millions of years. We don't have that luxury anymore. We must start doing democracy. Making time to meet with each other. Creating new democratic spaces in our workplaces, professional groups and communities where we can openly discuss, debate and reflect on how we are implicated in the wider global issues and explore how those issues are reflecting back on our communities, our workplaces and our lives.

And we have to start developing alternative strategies. Stop looking for 'experts' and easy answers, for heaven's sake! The experts don't really know and there *are* no easy answers. There are no maps of the future. We simply must start taking responsibility and sharing responsibility for bringing about a better kind of world and make our map as we go, by *learning* our way into the future, by asking great questions, being willing to experiment, willing to fail, and willing to learn. And by knowing that learning is messy, and real change is messy too.

It's a bit like spinning a web. As far as we know the spider has no plan. No concept of the wider context or the final structure. The web is truly emergent because the spider, working with a few simple but fundamental principles, simply interacts with what she has previously constructed and responds to what she meets. In human systems, those fundamental principles are our values.

And it's important to change our concept of change itself. In *Empowering the Earth*, author Alex Begg says: 'Revolution is not a spectacle, it's something we participate in. And it is neither fast nor sudden. It's slow, it's piecemeal, and it's mundane. Just like the destruction of the earth itself, it's the cumulative day-to-day actions of millions.'

In other words, deep change is not a firework display.

Inside our organisations we have to start taking our wider responsibility seriously, and recognise that corporate values shape decisions, and decisions shape landscapes and lives.

Perhaps we could ask: 'If we were to internalise the full cost of what we do, as well as the profits, would it still be profitable? When all the sums are done, is the difference we make a net positive?' The only way organisations will find out, is to loosen their sense of where their boundaries are, and widen the range of voices and perspectives that shape fundamental strategies. As the reality of our current ecological and social dilemmas begins to bite, the hard core financial case for responsible practice is getting stronger.

All of this requires that we get radical, wherever we are. I don't mean dying your hair pink (unless you'd really like to) or breaking windows at demonstrations. I mean 'getting to the root' of the matter. And the root of all of it is in here. It's in me. It's in you. It's the values, the beliefs and the assumptions that shape the behaviours, that shape the world.

Notes

1   In developing this framework of power I have drawn on the ideas of many thinkers, especially Stephen Lukes in *Power – A Radical View* (Palgrave, 1974), Alex Begg in *Empowering the Earth* (Green Books, 2000), Michel Foucault discussed by Barry Smart in *Foucault, Marxism and Critique* (Routledge and Kegan Paul, 1983) and Macy and Brown in *Coming Back to Life: Practices to reconnect our lives, our world* (Gabriola Island, New Society Publishers, 1998).

2   This idea is explored by David Edwards in *Free to be Human* (Green Books 1995) in commenting on the propaganda model put forward by Noam Chomsky and Edward Herman in *Manufacturing Consent*. Edwards comments that the [propaganda] model is intended to account for a dramatically effective system of control by which dominant interests are able to manipulate media behaviour from the broadest strategy down to the minutest detail of stress and intonation in individual journalistic reporting. A system of control which, he argues, is far tighter than anything imagined by Orwell or practised by totalitarian governments.

3   In relating Chomsky and Herman's argument that maintenance and control over the media and society generally doesn't necessarily require conscious planning (though this does happen), but simply happens as a result of 'free market' forces operating to meet the needs of the day, Edwards (ibid.) draws on an old school chemistry experiment designed to demonstrate the formation of crystalline structures.

4   Begg, Alex (ibid.) p. 247.

TIME TO CHANGE: HOW CAN WE DO THINGS DIFFERENTLY?
LEARNING FROM THE CONFERENCE MURAL

Paula Downey

The organisers of the annual Céifin conference have always struggled with how to include in the final book form the ideas and contributions of all those who make their way to Ennis each year.

When they asked if I would try to somehow include the workshop proceedings in this book, I said 'Sure!', but secretly wondered how on earth I would do it, or if it was appropriate to even try. After all, the purpose of the workshop was to mirror one of the central messages I'd been trying to communicate in my presentation on systems, power and change: that non-linear systems – including the system in the room, the conference itself – are largely *un*predictable, *un*manageable, *un*measurable, and *un*knowable.

In a world where there are no simple solutions to complex problems, where nothing is certain, no one's in charge, and nobody knows for sure how to proceed, the only realistic way to address the dilemmas at the heart of the conference is to participate, share responsibility and learn our way into a better place.

The workshop was an invitation to rethink change from a systems perspective and consider how we can all 'make difference' in relation to the issues that concern us. And the intention was to take a systems approach to the workshop itself – not to impose order on the process, but to give people an opportunity, however modest, to practise self-organising and sharing responsibility, both of which are essential if we're to take a systemic view of our dilemmas, and exercise our power to bring about change.

So that's what happened. The conference self-organised into groups and formed their own discussions on how to 'make difference' at different levels of the system – in our personal lives, in our workplaces and organisations, and in our communities. Afterwards, the delegates created a mural on the walls of the main room, to share their insights with all of those present.

Attempting to summarise workshop discussions at conferences like this is in many ways a denial of systemic truths. Whatever happens, happens. The experience is different for everyone so there's no single meaning, and often the real substance is deeply personal and private. Afterwards, it can't be neatly explained and even our best attempts are frequently a cardboard cut-out of what was a dynamic and often fascinating discussion. In my experience, the effects of a meaningful idea or conversation can be very subtle. Much later, when the inner system has had time to do its work, or when another thought or conversation or experience has been added to the mix, a comment that may have seemed insignificant at the time can become the catalyst for a major shift in perspective.

All of this still leaves me with a problem: how to fulfil my commitment to see that the substance of the workshops finds its way into this account. So, rather than impose my summary on discussions I wasn't part of, I've opted for a systems approach. I've gone up a level to 'see the whole thing' – to identify the patterns of thinking and the relationships between the key ideas that emerged, and tried to capture what the delegates' insights might teach us about the reality of change, and how we can do things differently.

The overlap of thinking between groups creates an overwhelming impression of synchronicity of thought. Interesting, isn't it, that dilemmas can appear intractable, and the possibility of massive change seems too audacious to contemplate. Yet in a matter of hours a couple of hundred people thinking freely together can come to some pretty similar conclusions about how to proceed.

Change is nested and personal
Whether people were discussing individual change or change at the level of the organisation or the community, a central theme emerging is that all change is personal. In fact, the contributions illustrate clearly that it's almost impossible to speak about system change without speaking about personal change in the same breath.

Considering how to trigger change in our wider social systems inevitably suggests some change in the life posture: changing our attitudes, changing our behaviours, changing our habits and practices, making different choices, altering our lens or perspective in some way.

A companion theme is that just as systems are nested within each other, change seems to be nested too. Personal change triggers change elsewhere in the system because our personal, community and organisational domains overlap and combine. The wider system shapes what individuals do, of course, but the assumptions and rules at the heart of the system are created by people. And in turn, people can choose to accept, abide by and defend them ... or question, renounce and recreate them.

Change is a journey
The mural tells us that deep change is a journey, not a single step, and the journey is circular. Or rather, iterative.

It seems to begin by updating a common feeling of powerlessness with a more accurate assessment of our personal power. Feeling power*ful* rather than power*less* triggers a sense

of personal responsibility, which in turn moves us to act –
personal power ... fuelling personal responsibility ... fuelling
personal action. This seems to be the trajectory.

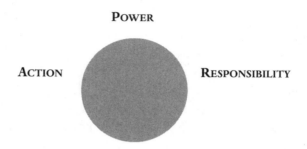

The journey is circular and iterative because the moment we
act on our convictions, our sense of power is amplified and a
virtuous circle is put in motion: the more powerful we feel, the
more likely we are to feel personally responsible in a situation
and compelled to act, and that action in turn fuels our sense of
power, heightens our sense of responsibility and drives us to act
again, and again, and again.

Personal power and change

Scanning the mural you can almost feel the power bubbling up
and flowing from the inner to the outer world – it's clear that
the impulse to create change is rooted in a belief in our power
as agents of change.

Of course the dominant system requires us to feel quite the
opposite, and to go quietly, but the conference said, '*No!* We have
to battle apathy – "*the great enemy*"– and fight cynicism, "*because
it's too easy to hide there*"'. Instead, we choose to participate
mindfully in our world and use our power in creative ways. We
recognise the power that lies in the smallest act accomplished
with integrity. We see the power present in every moment and in
every relationship. We swap docile followership in our various
communities for an authoritative membership. We stop seeing

ourselves as nay-sayers on the fringe and self-identify as participants in a vibrant interconnected global network of people who believe in something quite different than the world view on offer in the mainstream.

By trusting in our personal capacity to effect change we harness the latent power of the seemingly 'powerless'. Brazilian educator Paulo Freire, says that trusting the people is indispensable for revolutionary change. This conference added a rider to that: people also need to trust and believe in themselves.

Personal responsibility and change

In a system, you can never find the end of the ball of string, so the frantic search for someone to blame for our woes is ultimately futile. We may point the finger, but at best we're looking at a partial answer.

Truth is, whatever the problem, we're part of it in some way so, like it or not, we're also part of the solution. This means that often, *'change can't happen without us'*. It's not something we can leave conveniently to someone else. It becomes *'our moral responsibility'*, no matter where we perceive ourselves to be located on whatever pyramid we think we're clinging to.

In an interconnected, relational world, *'indifference is not allowed'*, because *'silence is sanction'*. Personal responsibility is about acknowledging that in every situation we have a role. And we have a choice.

These reflections are intimately linked to issues of truth and courage. Being willing to take a risk, willing to be different, willing to stand out and apart. Being brave and open about our values when it comes to making decisions *'even if that means saying "No"'*. Caring less about what other people may think of us, and caring more about what we're creating as we go.

'We need to be hurt into action!'; 'we're not desperate enough!' For those of us who are aware at some level that a web of spin and half-truths maintains the illusions that keep us mute or complacent, personal responsibility also means educating

ourselves and others, actively seeking out alternative sources of information, especially when that information is likely to discomfort us. It's not good enough to claim ignorance. We have a responsibility to look harder, to see further ahead than we're usually encouraged to, and acknowledge what we often turn away from.

Taking action for change

The patterns within the mural suggest that overcoming our sense of powerlessness and discovering our responsibility to act, is the hard part. After that, the answer to the question 'What can I *do* to bring about change?' seems likely to come more easily, and to evolve over time.

Of course, taking action of any kind to create the world we'd like to see builds our courage, capacity and resilience, and strengthens the foundation upon which we stand. Once we appreciate this, no act is puny, and what may appear to be a small act can hold within it a deeply political intention to alter the system in subtle, hidden ways.

'Voice' is a consistent theme ... voicing our values, voicing our concern, voicing our opposition, liberating ourselves to speak and act on our convictions, refusing to be silenced or to silence ourselves, speaking out courageously for what we believe. Never letting the moment pass, because we appreciate that this moment is connected to a million other moments. And there is no small act.

Writing about The Law of Action, Dan Millman says that 'No matter what we feel or know, no matter what our potential gifts or talents, only action brings them to life. Those of us who think we understand concepts, such as commitment, courage, and love, one day discover that we only know when we act; doing becomes understanding.'[1]

In whatever guise or forum we find ourselves, taking action consummates the power and responsibility assigned to us, and the delegates identified some of the many forms action can take:

Asking provocative questions. Challenging power. Saying no. Taking risks. Listening, especially to difference. Admitting 'I don't know' and making way for genuine dialogue and new conversations to take place. Respecting and involving other voices. Thinking outside of the box. Refusing to simply go with the flow. Questioning the 'experts'. Networking more. Encouraging others. Supporting alternatives – ideas, organisations, publications, products, candidates. Consuming less, reflecting more. Unplugging from thoughtless behavioural patterns. Choosing more consciously. Connecting more purposefully. Loosening control. Participating fully as active citizens 'doing democracy'.

Most of all, perhaps, eschewing the personal glory that often accompanies change agency, and choosing a quieter road ... prodding, provoking and disturbing the system into changing itself.

Change emerges

Finally, the mural teaches me that this rather hackneyed word – 'change' – is not something we can easily label, or point to, or even agree on. It's actually the emergent property of a circular, iterative process. A journey, rooted in a sense of personal power, driven by a sense of personal responsibility, that culminates in practical actions. And while our actions may seem modest relative to our ultimate ambitions, every time we act on our convictions we weaken the forces that keep us complacent, and increase our effectiveness as powerful, responsible and engaged creators of the world we experience.

References
Millman, D. (1995) *The Life You Were Born to Live*. CA: HJ Kramer/New World Library. p. 390.

LOCAL VISION FOR CHANGE

Padraig O'Ceidigh

I am going to share the Aer Arann story with you. But my purpose is not just to tell the story of Aer Arann, but rather to explain how it grew from small beginnings, and to outline the basic philosophies and principles that help me to run a successful business.

Whenever I am invited to speak, what really makes the experience a success for me is the people. Every person can go away and say: 'I developed a new idea from that' or 'What that guy said triggered something off in my mind.' I got involved in Aer Arann in 1994. My background is in teaching. I loved teaching; I was passionate about teaching. I left it because I had problems in the staffroom, but I never had problems in the classroom. Eventually, I just couldn't hack it. I needed to do something different. However, I learned a lot about people when I was teaching, things that stand to me in my business; I used to get my Leaving Cert. maths students to write their own maths book. Why? With all due respect to all those fine people who write maths books for the Leaving Cert., they never sat in a classroom with my students. They don't know how they think. If you write your own book, by God, you will remember it.

The story of my involvement in Aer Arann really began at Christmas, back in 1994. Every Christmas morning I go for a swim in Spiddal with my brothers. We have been doing this for years. Then we go to my parents' house. On Christmas night we go to visit my mother-in-law. This particular Christmas, I went for a walk. You know when you want to go off on your own at four o'clock in the evening? Well, on my walk I stumbled across an area that I had never explored before and discovered that they were building an airstrip on a bog in Connemara. You can imagine how it looked, with the mist coming down and it getting dark. I walked up and down that half-finished airstrip. Rocks, three-inch quarry stones and some tarmac. I began to get the idea that there was something magical about this. I ended up buying the airline.

I didn't have the money to buy it. I had very little money. But money never stopped me. Don't make money your problem. It is not about the money, it is about conviction. None of the banks would give me the a loan to buy the company, so I remortgaged my house. I had another site and I mortgaged that. Then I bought the company. The turnover at that time was about €250,000 a year. Eight years on, it is about €65 million. I did that without any bank loans, with banks believing I was stone mad, with people thinking 'What the hell does this guy from the middle of Connemara think he can do?'
When I started out I knew nothing about the aviation industry, not the first thing. People asked me 'Why did you buy it then? You can't go into something you know nothing about.' You know what I knew about? Teaching gave me this – I knew about people. Who runs airlines? Not aeroplanes, but people. I have an Irish language newspaper, Foinse. I am not a writer, but I work with people. People do the writing. People fly the aeroplanes. People create communities. I am involved in a whole lot of different businesses. They are very different. People say, 'How can you get involved in so many different businesses?' It is not the business, it is the people. It doesn't matter what you do. It matters who you do it with.

The vision I had for Aer Arann back in 1994 and 1995 was for it to become a safe, reliable, profitable service to the Aran Islands. Back then, we were flying about five thousand passengers a year. Now we have over 700,000 passengers a year. For the past three years we have been the fastest growing regional airline in the world. And why shouldn't the fastest growing regional airline in the world fly out of Connemara? Pretty quickly we achieved our goals. We were safe. We were profitable. We were reliable. Aer Arann was set up in 1970 and for the first time since 1970 the company started making profit. Yes, I had to be clinical, and I had to be tough, and I had to make decisions that weren't easy, but I made them. If you know in your gut something is right, just do it. The only times I made mistakes were when I didn't go with my gut feeling.

Then I wanted to create an internal airline in Ireland. Aer Lingus couldn't continue to be all things to all people. The only way I could do that is if I got certain government contracts, so I bid for them. I didn't get them the first time, thank God. But I got them the second time. Can you see the vision changing? Avoid getting stuck in the mud with the same vision. Move it on. It really bothers me when some big companies are so inflexible about their vision. They have it set in stone, written up in reception or up over the front door. Vision changes, because life changes. Your vision five years ago is different to what your vision is today, and it will be different in five years time. Let it change. Allow it to change. Support it to change. I knocked on the door of Aer Lingus. They told me to go away. I kept knocking and they still told me to go away, but I kept going.

Once we became Ireland's internal airline the vision moved on. Now, our vision is to be the best international regional airline in the world. Not necessarily the biggest, but the best. We are going to get there. We are going to keep going, keep going, keep going.

I ran the New York City Marathon last Sunday. The weather was 80 degrees out there. It was freak weather. I was going well in training out there. About twenty miles I got dizzy, disorientated, all the runners were going one way and I was going the other way. It wasn't easy. It was tough. I had a splitting headache, I was sick, but I kept going. I was going to finish that marathon if I had to travel the last six miles on my hands and knees. I wasn't doing it for anybody else. I was doing it because it was something I really wanted to achieve. I was going to keep going, keep going, keep going, no matter what. That ability is in every single one of us. It is just a matter of letting it get out.

That was the Aer Arann story in a nutshell. That was the 'what', and this is the 'how'. Imagine a hill, or better still, imagine Croagh Patrick or a big mountain. Imagine you have a gigantic ball that you have to push up the mountain. This is the story of Aer Arann in a different way. Imagine that you are pushing this huge ball up the mountain. Everybody thinks you are bloody mad. Everyone thinks you will fail. Nobody gives you money or support. When I took a career break from teaching, we all went for a night out. They were all saying: 'Fair play to you.' But I remember overhearing two guys talking about me. They were saying: 'Who the hell does he think he is? He will be back here next year, teaching. He is going out there thinking he is going to change the world, but he is going to come back to the safe, secure, teaching job.' It really hurt me. I went back in the bar area, and these two lads called me over saying: 'Padraig, you are the man. More power to you. You have guts. You'll make it happen.' And for years and years I was asking myself 'What happens if I fail? What if those guys were right. What happens if the ball comes down on top of me and crushes me?' But you know what? It's not about what other people think. You do it because you want to do it. It is your vision. You have a contribution to make. You decide what that contribution is from you. Not because somebody else says: 'Oh, he can't make it.' I don't feel that I have to make it just to show those guys they were wrong.

So you are pushing that ball up the hill and there are days when it is raining, and you slip back and the ball comes back a little bit. There are days when you can push a little further. But as you push it up a little bit, you know what happens – you start to get people in to help you push it up the hill. You get a little support and it gets easier. Sometimes there are little pebbles and sometimes big rocks in your way. They put you back a little bit, but you manage to weave around them or even push the ball up over those rocks. I believe that most businesses fail because they give up too early. They give up just that close to the 26.2 miles of the marathon; they are in Central Park, but they don't finish the race. They don't see the finish line because they give up too early. The don't go around the corner.

Have you ever felt that there was someone else on the other side of the ball, pushing it back down on you? That is the toughest part of it, not the rocks. Begrudgery. It is something I am not going to focus on.

Kieran McGowan – who is regarded as one of the main architects of the Celtic Tiger, although I know he doesn't like that term! – once told me a story. Whether it is true or not, it is very good! He was out in New York, in Greenwich Village, trying to get American companies to set up in Ireland. I organised a dinner for them at the best fish restaurant in Greenwich Village; they were sitting beside the lobster pond, and Kieran noticed that one of the lobsters was trying to climb out. The lobster was spilling water out the side and onto the table, so he called the waiter and asked if they could move to another table. And the waiter said, 'No there's no problem. You're all right there. They are Irish lobsters!' Kieran said, 'How do you mean they are Irish lobsters?' The waiter said, 'They do that every night. One of them goes so far and the rest of them will pull him back into the water after a while!' Be ready for begrudgery and accept it.

Imagine that inside the ball there are three cogs. One of those cogs we will call people. There are two parts to this cog. One part of it is called 'leadership'. You have to have a leader. A leader must be somebody with very clear vision. Somebody who can relate to his or her team. Someone with integrity, someone you can trust, someone who will walk the talk and talk the walk. There are leadership qualities in all of us. We all lead in different ways – be it in our families, our friendships, in the local GAA club, or the junior football team. It is just a matter of allowing that leadership ability to come out and of believing in what you are. The second part of that cog called people is 'the team'. The best way I can describe this is with a story from when I was a young lad.

We were playing football in Spiddal and we were really passionate about it. We got to the county final in football – a huge thing in Spiddal. I was about sixteen or seventeen years of age and I was playing right hand forward in the football team. We trained three times a week. There were beautiful young girls coming from Dublin and Waterford and all over the place to the Irish College in Colaiste Conaill. It was a serious sacrifice for us, not going to the Céilí and asking the girls up for the Walls of Limerick. We didn't go. No alcohol, no girls, no nothing, other than training. We won the county championships. We made it up with the girls soon afterwards. But that is not the story. The real story is that we went senior. We lost every game senior. It dawned on me three or four years ago why we lost every game senior. Why? With all due respect, there are many junior footballers even though it is the same game, the same pitch, the same ball the same rules, who never make it on a senior team. They just cannot adapt. I have had to change my Aer Arann management three times in the past four and a half years. I had to give them different jerseys. My goalkeeper probably went to the subs bench. My midfielder maybe went corner forward. You change around. You have to change around the team. It is the most difficult thing to do in life and in business.

The second cog in the wheel is information. People have to have the right information at the right time to make the right decisions. If you can, think of the third cog as a venn diagram, with three parts to it. Three circles. One circle is called passion. Whatever you do just have passion for it. If you are half hearted about it, get out. The second circle in the venn diagram could be called 'aptitude': do only the things you can actually be the best at. I know well and true that I wouldn't be the best at singing songs, or dancing. But I know I have a flair for working with people. I employ more than three hundred and fifty people. None of them work for me. They all work with me. The third circle might be called the 'barometer' or 'audit'. Have a couple of audit methods just to gauge how you are going along because very often you could be on the road from Ennis to Galway with a map. You can say: 'I would be better off if I take a different road or go a different direction'. Life is like that. Allow yourself to be changeable and flexible.

So in summary, push that ball up that hill. Create a vision that changes as you want it to change. It happens to all of us that sometimes the ball is pushed down against us. Accept it. Remember the three cogs. First: people, leadership and the team. Have the right people in the right positions with the right jerseys on them. Second: information. Third: the venn diagram – have passion for what you do, make sure you are doing what you are best at, then assess your performance, have a little bit of a self-audit. I ran the New York marathon in 1999 for two reasons: to raise money for Our Lady's Hospital for Sick Children in Crumlin, and for myself. I felt that if I could run a marathon, I would be able to grow an airline. Isn't that amazing? Just set little goals for yourself.

GLOBAL VISION
FOR CHANGE

Jim Power

I would first of all like to thank you for the privilege of addressing this conference. I have watched it with great interest since 1998 and have all the books of conference papers published by Veritas. When the opportunity to get up on the podium here at the Céifin Conference presented itself, I jumped at the opportunity. I am privileged, and I hope I can do it justice at such short notice.

Conferences such as this encourage debate and divergent views on a wide range of topics and this is very healthy. I worked for nine years as chief economist at Bank of Ireland. For about two years before I left I was getting increasingly frustrated because, in my view, the manner in which many large institutions are run forces self-limiting beliefs on the employees. I felt that every time I put my head above the parapet and expressed a view that was slightly right or left of the mainstream thinking within the organisation I got my hand firmly slapped. This conduct tends to characterise many aspects of Irish life and stifles real debate and innovative thinking. It is not healthy.

Today I have been asked to address how things have changed globally over the past decade or so, but I will also try to identify what I would regard as the key themes for the global economy and for the Irish economy over the next ten years. Before I start I should apologise to anybody I am about to annoy, but that is an inevitable consequence of debate. I have written a lot recently about the trends in Irish agriculture and the growth of part-time farming, which I don't believe is a good idea for the mainstream industry. I have attracted a huge level of opprobrium from within the agricultural industry. I got a letter from the minister, Joe Walsh, who told me I was giving a bad name to economists! I have also been very vocal over the last twelve months on the benchmarking issue. I am totally opposed to the whole concept, as it has been constituted. I am not arguing that teachers and nurses should not be better paid, but rather about the whole manner in which the benchmarking agreement was reached. This has not made me popular with public servants, but some things have to be said.

The past decade has been primarily dominated globally by the post-Cold War adjustment. Back in the late eighties we witnessed the fall of the Berlin Wall, and we have seen the story gradually evolve from then. From year to year it is branching off in very different directions and has had a profound impact on the balance of global power.

Arguably, the mess in Iraq at the moment is one further manifestation of the post-cold war environment. American hegemony is arousing considerable hostility and previous friends of the US have become enemies of that regime.

In Europe, the demise of Germany has been a key feature of the past decade. As well as coming out of the Cold War period, Germany has also had to shoulder the burden of reunification and is still struggling very badly with it, largely because at the time of reunification – and for very good reason – politics totally dominated economics. Very often outcomes represent a victory for politics over economics, but such outcomes inevitably leave a difficult legacy.

One of the difficulties about the world of economic forecasting and analysis in which I operate is that we are expected to be able to forecast the future. If we were able to forecast the future we would all be at it and it could prove very profitable. However, the problem with economic forecasting is that, very often, political realities take precedence over economic imperatives and can have a profound impact on the economic outcome. That is the world of *realpolitik*. I accept that world, but it makes it difficult to try to forecast the future. German reunification did not start off on a very sound economic basis and Germany has struggled subsequently with that process. It has become very obvious in Germany over the last ten years that the social and economic model that was created after the Second World War has long passed its sell-by date. It was very effective for quite a long time, but over the last ten or fifteen years it has failed to work. The political leadership is not strong enough to adjust the model and react to changed circumstances. At the moment, Germany is struggling very badly. It has 10.5 per cent unemployment. It is in serious industrial decline. If you look at German growth statistics over the last four decades, from decade to decade the average growth rate has been declining steadily. It is still a wealthy country based on past economic success, but unless economic growth is re-ignited, that wealth will gradually dwindle away. Over the next ten years Germany threatens to remain a model of economic and social underachievement.

The creation of the Single European Currency has been a major achievement for Europe in the 1990s and has brought to culmination the visions of many old Europeans. Politically EMU represented a major achievement against all of the odds; economically it has not, in my view, been a success, but there is still a long way to go. EMU is a very good example of politics winning out over economics and it remains to be seen how this will unfold. I am not terribly confident.

The biggest trend that we have seen in the UK over the last ten years has been a political one rather than an economic one. Britain has become almost a single party state. Since Margaret

Thatcher left power the Conservative Party has torn itself apart. There is now very little real political opposition and democracy has suffered as a result. I think the mess that Tony Blair got himself into during the Iraq war is indicative of the political vacuum that currently threatens that country and that body politic. I would like to see a strong Tory leader coming in and establishing a viable opposition because every political system needs that. Economically, Britain has done very well under Blair and has in many ways become a good political model of economic stability. This is no mean achievement.

Russia has come through a very interesting decade also. The ongoing attempt to try to replace the old communist elite is proving difficult and painful. It has resulted in situations where a lot of the old authority has fallen apart and illegal activities have filled the vacuum. However, one now senses that Russia is starting to come back on the radar screen as a place in which industrialists may seek to invest. Russia has a lot of positive attributes, not least the Russian people who are very bright, very educated and very capable. The future looks challenging, but bright, for Russia.

It has been a good decade for Asia. I am very pro-globalisation and I dismiss offhand many of the anti-globalisation arguments that are now in vogue. Asia is definitely a beneficiary of globalisation, not a victim. The economic growth performance in the region over the last ten years has been very strong and China in particular is now taking over as one of the most vibrant regions in the global economy. I certainly believe that over the next two or three decades China really is where all of the action is going to be concentrated. This poses huge opportunities, but also huge challenges for the developed world.

Within the Asian area, Japan stands out in a negative way. In Japan, like in Germany, the old social industrial and financial model that the economy operated on for decades has fallen apart. But there is no political leadership willing to change the whole process. The Japanese economy continues to be in serious trouble and a serious under-performer. It is an economy that is haunted by an economically disadvantageous demographic profile. The population is ageing rapidly and there is a lot of pension liability coming down the road, but very little wealth being created to finance the ageing population. Socially and economically, Japan has serious difficulties to face over the next decade.

Over the past decade, the US has established itself as a real world power, both politically and economically. It has become *the* dominant economic and political superpower. Economically, it is just as well, because given the failure of the European and Japanese economic models over the last decade, it is clear if the US wasn't leading the way, then the world economy would have been a very depressed place.

From an Irish perspective the boom in the US economy has paid huge dividends in terms of attracting foreign direct investment. The US economic success story has benefited people worldwide, but particularly here in Ireland. This flies in the face of a view that is now rampant here in Ireland, but human nature being what it is forces many to bite the hand that feeds them. My personal preference would be for Bush to be kicked out in November of next year because economically he is not terribly impressive. Back in the Clinton era, the economics function was a central part of the power structure in Washington. Economics has really been sidelined under Bush and the whole focus is now on political and military domination. That story is obviously going to be one that will play out in very strange ways in the coming years. It is definitely going to lead to an increased rise in Islamic militancy, which is definitely a serious threat to world stability. The attacks on the World Trade Centre in New York on 11 September 2001 were just one symptom of that.

Looking at the issue of globalisation, I don't agree with most of the arguments of the anti-globalisation people. I was in

Seattle just after the riots back at the World Trade Organisation meetings a few years back. It struck me that the anti-globalisation movement was just another excuse to practise anarchy. We have seen it in Dublin recently in relation to the bin dispute and the May Day protests a couple of years back. I think there is an element in society today that just wants to take every opportunity to practise anarchy on the streets.

As a technical economist, I look at some of the arguments the anti-globalisation people are making and find them strange. The reality is that although we have seen a widening of the gap between rich and poor, there is no doubt that while the rich have been getting richer, the poor have also been getting richer. So while the gap may have widened, all boats are being lifted by this tide of globalisation. Darwin would have had a view on this. The only option would be to keep everybody poor, which is what many of the anti-globalisation bodies on the left appear to want.

Statistics from the World Bank show that economic development and economic welfare indicators have all risen almost everywhere over the last ten years. The world is not the poor place today that it was ten years ago. It may be more unequal in certain respects, but it is not a poor place. What is the alternative? You stop globalisation? You put an end to the emergence of China? You put an end to the emergence of developing economies in Asia? I don't think that is in the interest of anybody either from a social, political or economic perspective.

I think that one of the biggest failures of the last ten years has been the failure of Africa to develop. I am not sure why Africa has failed to develop, but at a practical level I do know that the issues of land rights and property rights are very serious and hinder economic progress. Until Africa sorts out the issue of property rights and achieves some semblance of political stability, it will fail to become a viable economic entity. Africa has also been a victim of a trend decline in commodity prices. Why has there been a real decline of commodity prices?

It is largely because of supply and demand. There has been a huge increase in the supply of primary commodities, reflecting improved technology. At the same time the developed world has seriously reduced its dependence on primary commodities. So that demand/supply gap has forced real prices down and as a result, the primary commodity producers like Africa have failed to develop and have become even poorer. This situation needs to be addressed in a meaningful way, both for economic and humanitarian reasons.

One of the most topical aspects of globalisation, and one that is going to become very relevant in Ireland, is the whole topic of outsourcing of jobs. At the moment, this is a serious issue in Mexico. They are losing manufacturing jobs to China, India and the rest of Asia. When an economy like Mexico starts to complain about losing manufacturing jobs because they are becoming less competitive it is time to sit up and take notice. However, Mexico is not unique.

Silicon Valley in California is now starting to lose IT jobs to India and China. These are not low-level manufacturing jobs in the IT industry. They are the higher-level jobs in research and development.

Ireland is not immune to these trends and is, in fact, hugely vulnerable to this trend towards outsourcing. Quite simply, there comes a point in a country's economic development where certain activities become uneconomic. Ten years ago it may have made sense to manufacture T-shirts in Donegal, but today the economic arguments for doing so are a lot less compelling. As a country develops and becomes wealthier, costs rise and wages rise. Economic development, in my view, is not worth a whit if wage levels are not rising; you need to increase wages to increase and improve living standards. It is a natural part of economic development, but we have been losing – and are going to continue losing – these jobs to China and India, which are the two economies I would identify as the greatest challenge in that regard.

How do economies like Ireland or the United States face up to the challenge of outsourcing? The answer is that we should seek to replace the lost jobs with higher quality jobs, or to use the awful cliché, 'move up the value chain'. The only way to do this is through the quality of the labour force. The key has to be an investment in human capital. The one way we can raise our productivity and raise our living standards is to invest in human capital. Charlie McCreevy has stood up on Budget Day and boasted that he has consistently brought the public finances in at or below target. But an examination of the manner in which this is being achieved gives some cause for concern. Resources are being taken out of education and infrastructure. These are areas that will undermine the competitiveness of this economy in the longer-term. Many of our primary schools are ramshackle and give children who are getting their first exposure to the education system a very poor impression. Third-level facilities are also being drained of essential funding for research and development, and the stupid decision to abolish third-level fees is largely responsible for this. It is not good. This kind of short-term management is not in the long-term interests of the country. We have to invest in people; we have to produce high quality individuals who will continue to make Ireland an attractive location in which to invest, both for indigenous and multi-national entrepreneurs.

I think the issue today is, do we stop globalisation? If we do, we in the developed world won't suffer unduly in the short-term, but longer-term we will. However, China, India, and the emerging nations would be the real victims. Of course, with power comes responsibility. It is up to our political leaders to ensure that globalisation proceeds in a controlled manner, and that the social and environmental, as well as the economic aspect of the process, are managed very carefully.

The question of sustainable economic development is a very interesting one. I recently heard a Fine Gael councillor on 'Morning Ireland' who put the whole issue in context. The councillor was giving out about An Taisce, saying that if An Taisce had their way during the Ice Age, they would have sought to preserve ice for future generations. That probably wouldn't have been terribly sensible! But the real question with sustainable development is whether we stop economic growth? If we do, we are all going to be poorer at the end of the day. The secret is to try to achieve that balance between economic growth and development that will enhance living standards everywhere while at the same time protecting the environment. It is easy to stand up and say that, how we are going to do it is much more difficult.

The Irish economy has been amazingly successful in recent years. We have seen unemployment fall from over 16 per cent of the labour force ten years ago to just 4.4 per cent today. This is a truly remarkable performance. Today, most people who are willing and able can get a job in our vibrant economy. Ireland has also recently for the first time facilitated the emergence of an entrepreneurial culture. People like Michael O'Leary and Padraig O'Ceidigh have really shown us what can be done, I genuflect at the altar of Michael O'Leary on a frequent basis. There is now a much greater acceptance that entrepreneurs are good; they are positive; they enhance living standards; they make life better for everybody. That has been one of the biggest positive factors that has come out of the Celtic Tiger period. Of course there are still many begrudgers out there, but such people who hate success in others will always be with us.

The younger generation of Irish people are just so positive about everything. Negativity isn't really in their lexicon. It's funny that when the US economy went into recession in 2001, there were a lot of people saying to me, 'It's great! We're going to see this young generation seeing a bit of recession. They'll find out what life is really like'. There was almost a sense of hope that the Irish economy would go into recession so that the young people of today would find out what life was like for those of us who graduated, for example, during the 1980s, when we had to emigrate. Thankfully, it hasn't happened. Thankfully, the economy has come through a very different global economic environment relatively unscathed. Provided we do the right things over the next five years, the future looks reasonably bright for this economy.

There are some key challenges that arose during the Celtic Tiger era that we need to address going forward. One would be the breakdown of authority, the problem of random violence on the streets, and the huge dependence on alcohol and drugs that is emerging. These problems – particularly alcohol abuse – are ones that the older generation has to take responsibility for. I found it quite amazing that just before the World Cup last year a debate was going on, and our Taoiseach was joining in, on whether the pubs should open at six or seven in the morning to allow people to get alcohol while they watched World Cup soccer. The whole culture of alcohol dependency in this country is absolutely nuts, and it is directly feeding into a serious drugs problem. That is leading to a breakdown of authority, and I think it poses a serious threat to the future stability of this country, this economy and this society in general.

It's amazing how photographs can often express situations so much more clearly than words. People's lasting memories of major events often come from photographs – a naked girl running for her life, her clothes burned off by napalm, brought the horror of the Vietnam War into homes all over the world, while the photograph of a starving child with a vulture on a tree behind him did the same for the Ethiopian famine of the 1980s. I think the photograph we saw recently of a youth in Limerick giving two fingers to the Irish justice system represented a major impasse for Ireland. Law and order has broken down and crime has become endemic in our society. This is going to be a serious issue over the coming years. The leadership in this country has failed us very badly over the last decade: the authority of the Church has been seriously undermined, the authority of the political elite has been seriously undermined and the authority of the business elite has been seriously undermined. If you take out these three pillars that we all respected in the past, you are left with a vacuum and the question is. 'How do we fill that vacuum? How do we re-establish leadership, authority and most importantly respect for property and for people?' At the moment the vacuum is being filled by undesirable elements in society.

The provision of public services is also a serious issue for Ireland going forward. I look at the pre-budget submissions from bodies like IBEC. They argue against higher taxes, be they personal or corporation taxes. They argue against higher indirect taxes on items like fuel, alcohol or cigarettes. They argue against everything, but they come up with no solutions as to how we can finance public services. The health service in this country is, in my view, an absolute disgrace. I was a victim of it recently and I found it quite frightening. Education is also starting to crumble, as indeed are most of the public services we rely on. This is primarily due to a lack of finance, but there is also a serious issue of mismanagement. We have to address these issues. How are we going to finance the provision of public services and how are we going to manage them? These are the reasons why I found the recent refuse dispute in Dublin so distasteful. We have to pay for those services if we want them at a high quality. That is the bottom line.

Another issue is the future of employment. I mentioned that Irish unemployment, at 4.4 per cent of the labour force, is still very low, but if you look at the qualitative trends in employment, there are grounds for concern. We are seeing an increasing reliance on low-pay, part-time employment, particularly in the services sector. We are replacing a lot of relatively high-skilled, reasonably well-paid jobs with a lot of part-time, lower-paid jobs. This is what has happened in the US over the last couple of decades. This probably is the greatest downside of the US economic renaissance. I read a book recently called *Nickel and Dimed* by Barbara Ehrenreich, who spent twelve months working in the low paid labour force in the States in places like Walmart and McDonalds, and the story she tells is absolutely frightening. There is a distinct danger that this is the direction we are going in this country. We need to be very careful about that.

In conclusion, I think that the issues I have touched on today are some of the big, global challenges for the future. We have to accept that with power comes responsibility, be it business, political or religious. We need strong management and we need strong political leadership. It is great in recent months to see three political leaders coming through, prepared to take up the leadership. I refer to Minister Mícheál Martin, in relation to the smoking ban, Seamus Brennan for what he is trying to do in terms of transport infrastructure and Martin Cullen, who, in my view, is handling the whole refuse issue very well. We need more of that political leadership. We need strong decision-making if this country is to become a viable social and economic entity going forward. Finally, I would say that we need to see the development of an indigenous economy. Over the next ten years we are going to see a continuing decline in the numbers of people working in agriculture. The question is what will become of these displaced workers? Will they be forced to go into the already congested cities? We cannot stand by and allow the rural economy be denuded of people and economic activity. In my view, the secret of rural economic development in the next ten years is to ensure that those people who are going to be displaced from the land have a viable local rural economy to absorb them. This is one of the biggest challenges facing rural Ireland going forward. The recent decision to introduce decentralisation of public servants is a step in the right direction. Let's hope that we have sufficient political leadership to see it through.

Are we forgetting something?

'Romantic Ireland's dead and gone, it's with O'Leary in the grave', was the poet's cry a century ago. On the cusp of the third millennium many people fear the death of the Irish sense of community. The concept of a caring society seems well-buried in the selfishness of consumerism and *mé-féin*-ism encouraged by the phenomenon of the Celtic Tiger.

These were the concerns that inspired Fr Harry Bohan to organise a conference on the theme 'Are We Forgetting Something? Our Society in the New Millennium' in November 1998. Topics addressed ranged from the human search for meaning, to the economic boom in context.

This provocative and incisive volume, ably edited by Harry Bohan and Gerard Kennedy, also includes the views of the three chairpersons of the conference: Marie Martin, John Quinn and Michael Kenny, and is interspersed with well-chosen poetic and spiritual reflections on the topics addressed.

ISBN 1 85390 457 0

€11.45

Are we forgetting something?

Our society in the new millennium

Edited by Harry Bohan & Gerard Kennedy

Working Towards Balance

There is growing consensus that corporate and market values now shape Irish society.

Economic growth is synonymous with progress. But economic activity represents only one facet of human existence. Its values are not the only values that prevail in society. As we begin a new millennium, our society must be challenged to wonder what direction it is taking. There is an obvious need to ensure that the agenda of the corporate world and the welfare of local communities can co-exist in a meaningful relationship.

These are the concerns that were addressed at the 'Working Towards Balance' conference in 1999, organised by Rural Resource Development Ltd, (now the Céifin Centre) the papers of which are published in this book.

ISBN 1 85390 474 0

€11.45

Redefining Roles and Relationships?

These annual conferences in Ennis are establishing themselves as an important date in the calendar and meeting a need for serious discussion about major social and ethical issues of the day.

Mary Robinson
United Nations High Commissioner for Human Rights

The papers presented at the third Ennis Conference in 2000 are collected in this book. The need to redefine roles and relationships in a rapidly changing society was examined in many areas of modern life.

Papers include: 'Contemplating Alternative Relationships of Power in a Historical Perspective', Gearóid Ó Tuathaigh; 'Rebuilding Social Capital: Restoring an Ethic of Care in Irish Society', Maureen Gaffney; 'Rise of Science, Rise of Atheism: Challenge to Christianity', Bill Collins; 'Social Justice and Equality in Ireland', Kathleen Lynch; 'Putting People at the Centre of things', Robert E. Lane; 'Why Are We Deaf to the Cry of the Earth?', Seán McDonagh; 'It's Just the Media', Colum Kenny

ISBN 1 85390 526 3

€11.45

gearóid ó tuathaigh
maureen gaffney
bill collins
kathleen lynch
robert lane
seán mcdonagh
colum kenny

edited by harry bohan
and gerard kennedy

redefining roles
and relationships
conference 2000

Is The Future My Responsibility?

Have we become helpless in the face of change or can we manage the future? More and more people talk about the emptiness of modern life, they wonder where meaning is coming from and what values are shaping us; they say it is not easy being young today in spite of the choices and the freedom. We cannot assume that if we simply sit back and comment the storm will blow over, or that we will return to the old ways. The fact is we are experiencing a cultural transformation, we are witnessing the passing of a tradition, the end of an era. Every day we hear questions like 'Why aren't they doing something about it?' or 'Who is responsible for this, that or the other?' It is time to ask: 'Have I got any responsibility for the way things are?'

Including contributions from Nobel laureate John Hume and internationally renowned writer and broadcaster Charles Handy, *Is the Future My Responsibility?* is the fourth book of papers from the Céifin conference, held annually in Ennis, County Clare, and published by Veritas.

ISBN 1 85390 605 0

€12.50

Values and Ethics

can I make a difference?

What are the values that we choose to prioritise and live by? What price are we prepared to pay for ethics? Is it enough to rely on the law as the minimum standard of acceptable behaviour? Ultimately, can one person make a difference?

These and other far-reaching questions are addressed in *Values and Ethics*, the fifth collection of papers from the Céifin conference which is held annually in Ennis, Co. Clare. Contributors include Professor Robert Putnam (author of *Bowling Alone*), sociologist Dr Tony Fahey, Bishop Willie Walsh and Dr Lorna Gold from the University of York.

There is a belief in Ireland that we have not adjusted to our new-found prosperity. In a society that measures almost everything in monetary terms, values and ethics are increasingly sidelined. We now face the challenge of taking our social growth as seriously as we take our economic growth.

This book gives hope that real change can begin with committed individuals who believe passionately that shared values can become a social reality.

ISBN 1 85390 658 1
€13.95

CONFERENCE 2004

Imagining the Future
Who will shape it?

West County Conference and Leisure Centre
Ennis, Co Clare

3rd – 4th November 2004

For further information please contact
Máire Johnston, Conference Co-ordinator
The Céifin Centre, Shannon Business Centre,
Town Centre, Shannon, Co Clare
Tel: 061 365 912/3 • Fax: 061 361 954
ceifinconference@eircom.net
www.ceifin.com